Cookin' with Cocky II

More than just a cookbook

Charlie & Alex Hawkins

Preface and Acknowledgements

In 2004 my wife, Charlie, and I published a cookbook titled <u>Cookin' with Cocky</u>. It was so well received we decided to follow it up with <u>Cookin' with Cocky</u> II.

This book is published with a similar format with the bulk of the recipes coming from fans such as you. We hope our readers will find all the recipes to be fresh and equally tasteful.

THANKS

Once again, Charlie and I would like to thank you Gamecock fans for your cooperation in making this book possible.

We also offer our thanks to Emily White, Tom Price, Steve Fink, Eddie Elmore and Andy Solomon for their help in putting this book together, and our thanks and appreciation to Stuart Whatley for traveling back and forth from Atlanta, Ga., Ed Allen for the great cover design and Noelle Orr for the design and layout of this book.

Our special thanks to you loyal and passionate Gamecock fans for sharing your recipes and picture with us.

Dedication

If I were to write a dozen books regarding U.S.C. football they would all be dedicated to the loyal and dedicated fans that have supported the U.S.C. program for 112 years of very mediocre football. You people have been short changed for far too long. All that is about to change. I know you all have been told that before, but this time you can bet on it.

Winning is a habit and it's a habit that Steve Spurrier learned early and well. When he chose to come here he knew our history and our record. Hell, he beat us badly every year. But I knew he was up to the challenge when he brought up the question "Why Not Us"? That is a question Gamecock fans have been asking themselves for over a hundred years.

At the conclusion of the victory over Florida last fall, Spurrier resisted being carried off the field by admonishing his team with "What are you people celebrating? We didn't win a conference or national championship, we only won a game. You people have got to get use to winning." The bar had just been raised.

So I'm telling you Gamecock fans to get ready for your pay back. Get use to winning because "Why not us" is finally going to be answered, and if Steve Spurrier can't win at South Carolina then I totally subscribe to the Chicken Curse Theory.

I rest my case.

Table of Contents

2006 Football Schedule

Aug. 31	at Mississippi State
Sept. 9	Georgia
Sept. 16	Wofford
Sept. 23	Florida Atlantic
Sept. 28	Auburn
Oct. 7	at Kentucky
Oct. 21	at Vanderbilt
Oct. 28	Tennessee
Nov. 4	Arkansas
Nov. 11	at Florida
Nov. 18	Middle Tennessee State
Nov. 25	at Clemson

Appetizers

A Real Daiquiri - Howard Hughes

Armadillo Eggs - Frank Beatty

Barbequed Party Franks - Susie & Heyward King

Black-eyed Pea Cocktail Balls - Frances Sloan Fulmer

Bourbon Wiener - Frances Sloan Fulmer

Braunschweiger Balls - Ruth Grantz

Breakfast Sausage Balls - Dick Harris

Kingdaddy's Gamecocks Margaritas - Ryan Ramsey

Buffalo Shrimp - Stuart Whatley

Cheese and Sausage Balls - Lorna Graves

Chunky Guacamole - Lynn Steedman

Cocktail Meatballs - Frances Sloan Fulmer

Crab Cake Appetizer - Linda & Mike Withrow

Crab Cake Batch - Linda & Mike Withrow

Crab Appetizer - Roy & Ginger McLaurin

Crispix Snack Mix - Frances Sloan Fulmer

Devil Cheese Chips - Frances Sloan Fulmer

Easy Chex Mix - Susan Watts

Frosted Pecans - Frances Sloan Fulmer

Golden Olives - Paul & Peggy Trussell

Green Wonders - Sheila Fulmer

Grilled Shrimp with Bacon and Jalapenos - Frank Beatty

Ham Pinwheel - Frances Sloan Fulmer

Hot Peanuts - Frances Sloan Fulmer

Hot Pepper Jelly - Linda & Mike Withrow

Jan's Fruit - Dean & Alice Flanburg

Judy's Sausage Balls in Sauce - Susie King

Kingdaddy's Godzilla Magaritas - Ryan Ramsey

Leslie Kirk Appetizer - Cheryl & Ken Wheat

Pineapple Cheese Ball - Frances Sloan Fulmer

Prosciutto Wrapped Figs with Gorgonzola and Walnuts - Hannali & Red Ferguson

Ritz Bits - Van & Susan Mullis

Rum Balls - Frances Sloan Fulmer

Salami Surprise - Robbie & Sam Vickers

Salmon Spread - Kathi & Jimmie Mitchell

Sausage Balls - Ruth Grantz

Smoked Sausage with Oysters - Mary Ella Wright

Susie's Smoothie - Susie King

A Real Daiquiri
Howard Hughes (Big Daddy)

Prior to 1960 few people drank these until it was publicized as President Kennedy's favorite aperitif; for a period after that it was a very popular beverage and with good reason—it's delicious. Historical tradition is Jackie had this recipe thumb-tacked on the wall of the White House kitchen.

    2 oz. white rum
    1 oz. lime juice (must be freshly squeezed—the juice
        from one lime is about 1 oz.)
    ½ tsp. simple syrup (recipe follows)

Mix ingredients, shake vigorously over cracked ice, and strain into a chilled glass. To make simple syrup (not easily found in stores; quick to make and this amount will last a long time):

    2 cups sugar
    1 cup water
    2 tbsp. of Karo light corn syrup

Mix all ingredients and bring to a light boil for about 5 minutes (double boiler recommended).

Armadillo Eggs
Frank Beatty

    20 canned, whole jalapeno peppers (whole
        pepperoncini peppers may be substituted)
    3 cups (12 oz) sharp Cheddar cheese, shredded
    2 cups (8 oz) Monterey Jack cheese, shredded
    1 lb. mild ground pork sausage (hot sausage can be
        used as well)
    2 cups all-purpose baking mix (Bisquick, flour or corn
        meal all work well)
    2 large eggs, lightly beaten
    1 package (6 oz) seasoned coating mix for pork

Cut a lengthwise slit on one side of peppers, leaving other side intact, and remove seeds. Stuff each pepper with sharp Cheddar cheese (about 2 teaspoons). Pinch edges to close and set aside.

Combine remaining Cheddar cheese with Monterey Jack cheese, sausage and baking mix. Pinch off about 2 rounded tablespoons of dough, shape into a ¼ inch thick patty. Place a stuffed pepper in center of patty and wrap dough around pepper. Dip in egg, dredge in seasoned coating mix. Place on a lightly greased 15x10 inch jelly-roll pan (a baking sheet with sides). Repeat with remaining dough and peppers; cover and chill up to 2 hours if desired.

Bake at 375° for 30 minutes or until golden brown.

This recipe makes about 10 appetizer servings.

Appetizers

HEYWARD KING

"The Lake City Flash" was a five-time letterman at USC in the late 1950's. He played baseball in his freshman year. He captained the track team earning three letters there and earned two more letters in football.

He joined his father in 1960 at the W. Lee Flowers Company, a wholesale grocery supplier in Lake City. They supplied to all the IGA stores in South Carolina. Since that time W. Lee Flowers and Company has grown. With Heyward as CEO they now supply all the IGA stores in South Carolina and some in Georgia and North Carolina. They now own 32 of the IGA stores here.

Barbequed Party Franks
Susie & Heyward King

2 lbs. wieners
1 can beer
½ cup barbeque sauce
1 cup brown sugar

Cut wieners 1 inch thick. Mix ingredients and pour over wieners. Marinate overnight. Cook over medium heat in saucepan for 30 minutes. They will expand. Serve with sauce and toothpicks.

Black-eye Pea Cocktail Balls
Frances Sloan Fulmer

1 15 oz. can black-eye peas, drained and mashed
2 tbls. grated onion
1 egg, beaten
1 tbls. salad oil
About 5 tbls. all-purpose flour
Ground red pepper to taste
¼ tsp. salt
¼ tsp. pepper
¼ tsp. sage
Salad oil for frying

Combine all ingredients, mixing well. Drop by rounded teaspoonfuls into hot oil; cook until browned. Drain on absorbent paper towels.

Yields about 2 dozen.

Appetizers

Bourbon Weiners
Frances Sloan Fulmer

4 12 oz. pkgs. Wieners
1 cup bottled chili sauce
1 cup bourbon
1 cup brown sugar

Cut wieners into chunks at least ½ inch thick. Combine other ingredients and pour over wieners. Bake covered at 350° for 45 to 60 minutes. Refrigerate at least over night so that accumulated fat may be skimmed off. To serve, reheat in oven uncovered on low heat. Put wieners in chafing dish along with a small amount of the sauce. Keep warm.

Ruth Grantz with Alex
and her son Jeff

JEFF GRANTZ

Second team All-American in 1975 and one of only three Gamecocks with more than 5,000 yards of total offense. An equally outstanding baseball player as he played shortstop and second base. Jeff played on three NCAA playoff clubs, including the 1975 team that advanced to the finals of the College World Series.

In a poll conducted by *The State* paper, Jeff was voted the best quarterback in the history of USC football .

A fierce competitor, there is nothing Jeff likes about losing.

Postgame Celebration at Arkansas, 2005

Braunschweiger Ball
Ruth Grantz

1 roll of Braunschweiger
½ cup grated onion
1 tbl. mayonnaise
Small pkg. of cream cheese

Mix all the ingredients. Roll into large ball. Ice with cream cheese softened with milk. Serve with your favorite crackers.

DICK HARRIS

Made all ACC and first team All-American in 1971. Dickie was the most exciting kick returner in the history of the school. He played 10 years of pro football in the Canadian League and he is a member of the University's Hall of Fame.

Breakfast Sausage Balls
Dick Harris

4 slices bread, cubed
2 tbs. freshly squeezed orange juice
2 tbs. maple syrup
1 egg, slightly beaten
½ lb. mild sausage meat
½ cup finely chopped toasted pecans
2 tbs. chopped fresh parsley

Soak bread in orange juice and syrup. Add egg and mix thoroughly. Blend in sausage, pecans, and parsley. Form into 1 inch balls. Fry over low heat, turning occasionally, 12 to 15 minutes, until brown.

KingDaddy's
Gamecock Margaritas
Ryan Ramsey

In a gallon jug combine the following:

1 liter Gold tequila (I prefer Sauza)
1 ½ cup Fresh squeezed lime juice. (Takes 10-12 limes)

1 small can Frozen Limeade
1 cup Water
1 cup Triple Sec
1 ¼ cup Orange juice
1/8 tsp. – ¼ tsp. Salt

Shake the first 7 ingredients in the jug. Then fill the jug with Wink*(takes most of a 2 liter bottle). Mix gently, and serve over ice.

Remember to stand up frequently between servings. If dizziness occurs, discontinue consumption.

Option: If you want a festive green color add 1 drop of green food coloring prior to step 2.

* This recipe is tailgating size at 1 gallon per hatch. The downside is that one of the items is not currently available in Columbia, but is in Charlotte and Atlanta. That secret ingredient, if you will, is WINK. It is a soft drink manufactured by Canada Dry. Around here the closest thing that I have found is Canada Dry Collins Mix, but that is a little sweet for my recipe.

Appetizers

Cheese and Sausage Balls
Lorna Graves

3 cups biscuit mix (such as Bisquick)
I lb. sausage
8 oz. sharp cheddar cheese, grated
I tbsp. water

Mix all ingredients together. If too dry, add I Tbsp. of water. Form into one inch balls. Bake on ungreased cookie sheet at 350° for 20 to 25 minutes.

Cheese Straws
(The Last Straw)
Lynn Steedman

I stick unsalted butter (softened)
½ stick Crisco vegetable shortening
I LB. extra sharp cheddar cheese, finely grated
2 ½ cups all purpose flour
I tsp. salt
I tsp. dry mustard
I tsp. red pepper (or to taste)

Pre-heat oven to 350°. Place butter and Crisco in large mixing bowl and cream until smooth. Gradually add cheese and mix well at medium speed. Combine flour, salt, mustard and red pepper in separate bowl. Add to cheese mixture in 3 additions, mixing well after each addition using low speed. Fill cookie press with dough and push onto greased cookie sheet...I use the ribbon disc.

Bake at 350° for 10-12 mins. Until edges are just starting to turn brown. Carefully remove and cool on wire rack or brown paper bags.

Buffalo Shrimp
Stuart Whatley

2 -4 lb. medium shrimp
2 bottles Texas Pete Hot Sauce
I stick butter
Box Zatarains Fish Fry
Oil to fry shrimp

Clean and devein shrimp. Follow directions for fish fry Dredge shrimp in mix and fry in hot oil. Drain fried shrimp of oil. Melt butter and add Texas Pete. Toss fried shrimp in hot sauce. Serve with celery and blue cheese dressing. Can substitute with oyster or calamari. ENJOY!

Appetizers

Chunky Guacamole
Lynn Steedman

2 Ripe Avocados
3 Green Spring Onions
Cherry or Grape Tomatoes
Mayonnaise
Fresh Lemon Juice
Chili Powder

This is an "Eye-Ball" recipe. You should peel and dice avocados into a bowl and squeeze half a lemon onto it. Cut tomatoes in half or quarter depending on size and you should add enough tomatoes to be about half and half with the diced avocados. Add diced spring onions, including part of the green. In another bowl mix a couple of blobs of mayo (enough for dipping consistency), squeeze other half of lemon and a sprinkle of chili powder. Pour this over the avocados, tomato and onions. Refrigerate until ready to serve. Dip with Tostitos, Fritos, or Doritos.

Cocktail Meatballs
Frances Sloan Fulmer

2 lbs. ground beef
2 eggs
½ tsp. salt
¼ tsp. pepper
1 large onion, grated

Combine all of the above ingredients and shape into tiny balls.
1 jar (12 oz.) chili sauce
1 jar (10 oz.) grape jelly
4 tsp. lemon juice

Combine and put in large baking dish. Add meat balls and bake at 350° for 1 ½ hours. Serve in chafing dish and provide toothpicks.

Crab Cake Appetizer
Linda & Mike Withrow

3 oz. crab cake batch, recipe follows
1 oz. frisee lettuce
½ oz. citrus beet vinaigrette
1 each endive leaf
1 oz. chili remoulade
¼ oz. dill oil
2 oz. cooked shredded potatoes
1/8 oz. all-purpose flour
1/8 oz. pasteurized eggs

In a fryer, fry the crab cake until golden brown. Dress the frisee lettuce with beet vinaigrette and place in ring mold in center of a plate. Remove mold and place crab cake on lettuce and top with chili remoulade and endive leaf. Paint plate with dill oil.

Crab Cake Batch

1 lb. crab meat
1 oz. mayonnaise
1 oz. egg yolks
1 ¼ oz. diced onion
1 ¼ oz. diced celery
2 oz. white wine
1 ½ oz. Panko (Japanese breadcrumbs)
1 tsp. Old Bay seafood Seasoning
Pinch white pepper
1 tbsp. Worcestershire Sauce
1 oz. Dijon mustard

Sweat the celery and onions in white wine. Add Old Bay seasoning and kosher salt and reduce until almost dry. In a bowl, blend with remaining ingredients.

ROY MCLAURIN

Roy was a teammate of mine back in the late 50's. He was a 180-pound guard that I honestly don't know how he kept from being killed.

Crabmeat Appetizers
Ginger & Roy McLaurin

Crabmeat
Onion, minced
Celery, minced
Some mayonnaise
Salt & Pepper to taste

If you're going to cook the crabs yourself, always make sure they are alive and wiggling! NEVER cook a dead crab.

Mix crabmeat with minced onion, celery and some mayonnaise—add a little salt and pepper to taste. Can be used as a sandwich filling, chilled as a salad, and delicious on crackers!!

Crispix Snack Mix
Frances Sloan Fulmer

1 large box Crispix cereal
1 cup powdered sugar
1 stick margarine
2/3 cup peanut butter
9 oz. milk chocolate (like a milk chocolate bar, i.e. Hershey's)
9 oz. semi-sweet chocolate chips

Put chocolate chips, milk chocolate, peanut butter and margarine in a bowl. Melt in microwave for 2-3 minutes (stir after 1 minute.) Just melt for long enough to soften ingredients so they can be easily stirred and mixed together. Pour ½ Crispix into a large bowl, then pour ½ of above mixture over the Crispix and stir carefully together. Repeat with the other ½ of Crispix and mixture. Pour powdered sugar over the top and mix all together (the powdered sugar makes it easier to break into small bite-size pieces.)

Deviled Cheese Chips
Frances Sloan Fulmer

1 cup finely crushed potato chips
1 ½ cups shredded cheddar cheese
2 (4 ½ oz.) cans Deviled Ham
1 cup all-purpose flour
¼ tsp. red pepper

Combine all ingredients, mixing well. Shape mixture into a 9-inch long roll; chill. Cut into ¼ inch slices. Bake at 425° for about 10 minutes.

Yields: 3 to 4 dozen chips

Appetizers

Easy Chex Mix
Susan Watts

5 tbls. butter
½ tsp. salt
6 cups of your favorite chex cereal
1/3 cup grated Parmesan cheese

Melt butter in large skillet over low heat. Stir in salt. Add cereal. Stir until all pieces are covered. Continue to heat and stir for 5-6 minutes or until cereal is lightly toasted. Sprinkle with cheese; stir to coat all pieces. Spread on paper towels to cool.

So delicious and easy!! I use a mixture of Rice and Corn Chex, but you can use your favorite type(s). May as well go ahead and make the entire box(es) of Chex Cereal, not just 6 cups!

Frosted Pecans
Frances Sloan Fulmer

1 lb. pecan halves
1 egg white
1 tsp. water
½ cup sugar
¼ tsp. salt
½ tsp. cinnamon

Beat egg whites and water until frothy, not stiff. Add pecans and mix well. Combine sugar, salt and cinnamon. Mix pecans in mixture until well coated. Bake 1 hour at 225° in shallow pan, stirring every 15 minutes.

Deviled Ham Puffs
Frances Sloan Fulmer

1 8 oz. package of cream cheese, softened
1 tsp. onion juice
½ tsp. baking powder
Pinch of salt
1 egg yolk
24 2 inch bread rounds
1 4 ½ oz. can deviled ham

Mix cheese, onion juice, baking powder, salt and egg yolk. Toast bread rounds on one side. Spread untoasted side with deviled ham. Cover with mound of cheese mixture. Bake on cookie sheet at 375° about 10 minutes. Serve warm.

Appetizers

Golden Olives
Paul & Peggy Trussell

1 cup sharp cheddar cheese, grated
2 tbls. butter, room temperature
½ cup flour
Dash of cayenne pepper
24 small to medium Pimento-Stuffed Olives

Preheat oven to 400°. In a small bowl cream the cheese and butter. Add flour and cayenne, blending well. Mold a teaspoonful of dough around each olive, covering completely. Place on baking sheet and bake for 15 minutes or until pastry is golden brown.

SPECIAL INSTRUCTIONS: I usually double this recipe. They are so easy to pop in your mouth and are gone in no time.

Green Wonders
Sheila Fulmer

2 (10 oz.) pkgs. frozen spinach, cooked and well drained
2 cups herbed stuffing mix
2 large onions, finely chopped
5 eggs, beaten
¾ cup margarine, melted
½ cup parmesan cheese, grated
1 tbl. garlic salt (or to taste)
1 ½ tsp. thyme
Black pepper, to taste

Mix all ingredients in bowl. Chill at least 2 hours. Shape into small balls and place on cookie sheet and freeze. As soon a frozen, remove and pack in container made for freezing. Remove as needed. To serve, put on ungreased cookie sheet. Bake for 20-30 minutes at 350°. Serve hot. Makes 70 to 90 serving.

Grilled Shrimp with Bacon and Jalapenos
Frank Beatty

16 thick round wooden picks (do not use the thin flat ones)
16 large fresh shrimp, unpeeled
2 jalapeno peppers
2 tbls. olive oil
¼ tsp. salt
1/8 tsp. pepper
8 thick-cut bacon slices, halved length-wise

Soak round wooden picks in water for about 30 minutes. Peel shrimp, leaving tails on and devein if desired. Set aside.

Cut each pepper lengthwise in 8 pieces; remove seeds. Toss together shrimp, jalapeno peppers, olive oil, salt and black pepper in a large bowl. Set aside. Microwave bacon slices on HIGH for 30 seconds.

Wrap 1 bacon slice around 1 shrimp and 1 jalapeno pepper slice. Secure with a wooden pick. Repeat procedure with remaining bacon slices, shrimp and jalapeno pepper slices. You should finish with 16. Grill, without lid, over medium high heat for 4 to 6 minutes or until shrimp turn pink, turning once. This recipe makes 8 servings. The preparation can be done a day or two ahead if you'd like to refrigerate the shrimp and grill them on game day.

Appetizers

Ham Pinwheels
Frances Pulmer

6 slices boiled ham
1 3 oz. pkg. cream cheese, soft
1 small bottle stuffed olives
¼ cup chopped pecans
1 tbl. mayonnaise
Dash Tabasco

Mix softened cream cheese with mayonnaise. Add chopped olives and nuts and Tabasco. Spread on boiled ham. Roll up ham and wrap in Saran wrap. Place in refrigerator or freezer. Slice rolls when ready to serve. Place cut side up on tray.

Hot Peanuts
Frances Pulmer

1 tbl. Ground red pepper
3 tbls. Olive oil
1 ¼ tsp. garlic powder
1 12 oz. can Cocktail peanuts
1 12 oz. can Spanish peanuts
1 tsp. salt
1 tsp. chili powder

Put oil in pan, add red pepper and garlic powder. Heat for several minutes, stirring to blend. Add peanuts and cook over medium heat for about 5 minutes. Remove from heat and stir in salt and chili powder. Drain well on several layers of paper towels.

Hot Pepper Jelly
Linda & Mike Withrow

1 cup fresh hot peppers
1 cup bell peppers
1 ¼ cup white vinegar
6 cups sugar
1 bottle of Certo-NOT Sure Jell
You can use any color of food coloring (red, green, etc.) to make it colorful.

Mix all ingredients in a blender except sugar and Certo. Add sugar and bring to a boil. Add Certo and boil for 1 minute. Take off the stove and skim the ingredients. Add coloring as desired and put in jars.

This is a great appetizer served with cream cheese and crackers.

Appetizers

Jan's Fruit
Dean & Alice Flansburg
Orangeburg Gamecock Club

Mandarin Oranges
Sliced Peaches
Sliced Pears
Pineapple Chunks
Instant Banana Pudding
Bananas sliced

Drain canned fruit: Place in serving bowl. Sprinkle Instant Banana Pudding, stir, and add sliced bananas before serving.

Judy's Sausage Balls In Sauce
Susie King

1 lb. ground sausage
1 pkg. cheddar cheese, finely grated
1 cup bisquick
1 large bottle Kraft barbeque sauce
4 tbls. Grape jelly

Mix sausage, cheese, bisquick and form 2 inch balls. Bake balls in a 350° oven for 30 minutes. Drain. Melt jelly in sauce pan and add barbeque sauce and heat. Put sausage balls in chafing dish with sauce. Serve hot.

Will Kirk

Leslie Kirk Appetizer
Cheryl & Ken Wheat

1 stick cream cheese
1 jar pizza sauce
Chopped red onion
Sliced Pepperoni
Sliced black olives
Mozzarella cheese

Spread cream cheese on bottom of pan. Add pizza sauce, red onion and black olives. Add cheese and pepperoni.

Bake in oven at 350° for 20 to 30 minutes.

Appetizers

Pineapple Cheese Ball
Frances Sloan Fulmer

2 8oz. pkg. cream cheese, softened
1 8 ½ can crushed pineapple, drained
2 cups chopped pecans, divided
¼ cup finely chopped bell pepper
2 tbsp. finely chopped onion
1 tbsp. seasoned salt

Beat cream cheese until smooth. Stir in pineapple, 1 cup of pecans, bell pepper, onion and salt. Shape into a ball. Roll in cup of nuts. Wrap in plastic wrap and chill over night. Serve with crackers.

Prosciutto-wrapped Figs with Gorgonzola and Walnuts
Hannalie & Red Fergson

9 large fresh figs, stemmed and halved
18 1x5" thin strips Prosciutto (about 3 ounces)
3 tbsp Gorgonzola cheese
18 large walnut pieces, toasted.

Preheat broiler. Cover baking sheet with foil. Wrap each fig half with 1 Prosciutto strip. Broil until Prosciutto chars slightly on edges, about 1 ½ minutes. Turn figs; broil about 1 ½ minutes longer, watching closely to prevent burning. Place ½ tsp Gorgonzola atop each fig half. Top each with walnut piece. Serve warm or at room temperature.

Ritz Bits
Van & Susan Mullis

2 boxes Ritz Bits with cheese
1 heaping tbl. dill
1 tsp. garlic powder
1 tsp. celery salt
1 pkg. Hidden Valley Ranch Dressing (dry)

Mix in a big bowl and refrigerate several hours.

Rum Balls
Frances Sloan Fulmer

2 ½ cups vanilla wafer crumbs
1 cup powdered sugar
1 tbsp. cocoa
1 cup ground nuts
3 tbsp. white Karo syrup
1/3 cup white Rum

Mix all well. Form into balls and roll in additional powdered sugar. Put in refrigerator to set.

Robbie Vickers

Appetizers

SAM VICKERS

Sam is Chairman of the Board and CEO of Design Container Corporation of Jacksonville, Fla. and they do business all over the world. He is on the Board of Directors of the South Financial Group. He was chairman of the Federal Reserve Board for six years and he also owns the finest collection of Florida art in the world.

Sam's wife, Robbie, was a cheerleader at USC in the late 50's. They live at the mouth of the St. John's River in Jacksonville. They have two daughters and six grandchildren. Is Robbie pretty or what?

Salami Surprise
Sam & Robbie Vickers

½ lb. Genoa Salami
1 lb. Cream cheese
1 Bunch fresh Asparagus
1 jar green olives

Cook asparagus until almost done but still firm. Spread softened cream cheese on slice of salami. Place one asparagus in the middle and roll up in salami. Cut into 1 inch pieces and secure with tooth pick holding with a slice of green olive on top.

This recipe will make quite enough for 10 to 12 people.

Bill Caine & Kathi Mitchell

Salmon Spread
Kathi & Jimmy Mitchell

1 can Salmon, boneless drained
1 tbsp. Lemon juice
2 tsp. Horseradish
¼ tsp. Tabasco
8 oz. Cream Cheese
1 tbsp. grated onion
¼ tsp. salt
¼ tsp. Worcestershire sauce

Mix together and chill. Shape into a ball and roll in slivered almonds or parsley.
Serve with crackers or sliced French bread.

Sausage Balls
Ruth Grantz

1 lb. hot sausage
3 cups Bisquick
8 oz. cheddar cheese

Mix all ingredients. Roll into balls. Bake at 350° for 15 minutes.

Smoked Sausage with Oysters
Mary Ella Wright

2 lbs. Country Smoked Sausage
1 qt. Medium sized Fresh Oysters
2 cups Sauterne Wine
1 tsp. Louisiana Hot Sauce
½ tsp. Salt
Juice from ½ lemon

Cut sausage in one inch pieces and place in large frying pan, preferably an iron pan. Add oysters, wine, hot sauce, garlic salt and lemon juice. Bring to a good boil, and then turn heat down so that it will cook slowly. Cook until ½ of juice is gone, leaving enough to serve as gravy. Be sure sausage is well cooked and tender.

Dip French Bread in sauce.

Susie's Smoothie
Susie King

2 or 3 bananas, peeled, broken up and frozen in a zip lock bag
2 cups milk
½ cup peanut butter, more or less
4 or 5 heaping tbsp. Chocolate Instant Breakfast

Put all ingredients in a blender until creamy. You can adjust the ingredients according to taste. Fruit smoothies can be made with any frozen fruit and any fruit juice you have on hand. These are refreshing, filling and good for you!

THE GAMECOCKS' No. 1 FAN

Breads

Baked Apple French Toast - Edith & Art Baker

Banana Nut Bread - Bobby Bryant

Beer Bread - Kathy & Gerald Sease

Billie's Vidalia Onion Cornbread - Steve Tanneyhill

Breakfast Pizza - Frances Sloan Fulmer

Cathead Biscuits - Billy Canada

Corn Bread - Mary Hughes

Dill Bread - Zoe & Alex Sanders

Dilly Casserole Bread - Susie & Heyward King

Easy Whipping Cream Biscuits - Susie & Heyward King

Hot Water Corn Bread - Keith Wright

Hush Puppies - Brad Edwards

New England Corn Fritters - Johnny Grambling

Patsy's Strawberry Bread - Ryan Brewer

Pumpkin Bread - Margaret & Ruddy Attaberry

Sesame Cheese Muffins - Todd Ellis

Art Baker

Art was born in Sumter, S.C. and played two years at Presbyterian College. He was the head coach at Eau Claire High School and coached for five years at Clemson under Frank Howard. Art spent three years at Texas Tech and was the head coach at Furman, 1971-78, and at The Citadel from 1980-82. He was at Florida State and East Carolina before coming to USC as a consultant to the Athletic Department in 1989 and remains there even as we speak.

Baked Apple French Toast
Edith & Art Baker

3 large green apples
1 stick (1/2 cup) butter
½ cup brown sugar
12 oz. cream cheese
12 slices firm bread
8 eggs
2 cups milk
2 tbl. vanilla
Cinnamon

Set rack in lower third of oven; preheat to 350°. Butter a 13x9 inch pan. Core and cut apples into thin wedges, leaving skin on; In skillet, melt butter with brown sugar and 1 tbl. of water. Add apples and cook, stirring for 2-3 minutes. Transfer cooked apples to baking dish; allow to cool; Cut cream cheese into cubes; arrange evenly over apples. Cut slices of bread diagonally; layer over apples; In large bowl, beat eggs, milk and vanilla. Pour egg mixture over bread. Sprinkle with cinnamon.

Bake 40 to 50 minutes until golden and puffed. Let cool for 10 minutes.

Bobby Bryant

In my mind and in many others, Bobby is the best athlete ever to attend the University of South Carolina. An All-American defensive back in 1966, his 98-yard punt return is still a school record. Drafted by the NY Yankees and the Boston Red Sox, he won the McKevlin Award in 1966-67 as the top athlete in the ACC. His 14 years as a starting cornerback for the Minnesota Viking is unheard of. Bobby has played in four Super Bowls and is, of course, in the state and school's Hall of Fame.

Banana Nut Bread
Bobby Bryant

2 sticks oleo
2 cups sugar
3 cups plain flour
2 tsp. soda
1 tsp. salt
6 very ripe bananas
2 cups pecans, chopped
2 tsp. vanilla
4 eggs

Cream butter and sugar. Add eggs, flour, soda, salt, vanilla, bananas and nuts. Line two loaf pans with waxed paper. Bake 1 hour at 350°.

Beer Bread
Kathy & Gerald Sease

3 cups self rising flour
3 tbsp. white sugar
12 oz. beer, any style
2 tbsp. butter

Blend flour and sugar in mixing bowl. Preheat oven to 350 degrees. Make a well in center of flour mix. Pour beer into middle and mix until just blended; Pour into buttered 9x5x3- inch loaf pan. Bake until done, about 50 mintues. Turn loaf out of pan. Cool on rack. Serve warm with butter.

Variations: Add ¼ cup sun-dried tomatoes, 1 tbsp. minced onion, ½ tsp. dried basil, ½ tsp. salt, ¼ tsp. garlic powder to the batter.

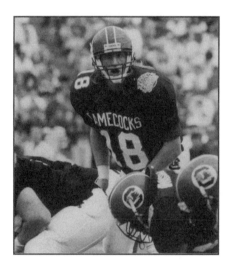

Steve Tanneyhill

Steve holds many school records including: net yards gained in a single game (512), passes attempted in one game (58), consecutive completions (18), passing yardage in one game (473), and passes completed in one game. He is first, second, third and fourth on other lists. His 3,094 passing yards in one season is second to Todd Ellis.

Breads

Billie's Vidalia Onion Cornbread
Steve Tanneyhill
Submitted by Billie Edwards

½ cup onion, grated
2 tbsp. butter
½ cup sharp cheddar cheese
½ cup sugar
1 pack jiffy cornbread mix
1 egg
½ cup sour cream
¼ cup virgin olive oil
1 tsp. salt
1/3 cup buttermilk

Cook onions in butter until tender and clear. Prepare mix according to package directions, adding oil, sugar, and salt. Pour into greased 8 x 8x 2 inch pan. Mix cooked onions, sour cream and cheese together. Spoon over top. Bake at 400 ° for 25 minutes or until done. Let stand a few minutes before cutting. Recipe may be doubled in a larger pan.

This is delicious with pinto beans in the winter and fresh butterbeans in the summer.

Breakfast Pizza
Frances Sloan Fulmer

1 pound Sausage
1 package Crescent Rolls
1 cup frozen, loose, Hash brown potatoes
1 cup Cheddar Cheese, shredded
5 eggs
¼ cup milk
1/8 tsp. pepper
½ tsp. salt
2 tbsp. Parmesan Cheese

Cook sausage and drain. Place dough in ungreased 12-inch pizza pan with the points to the center. Press the edges together to seal. Spoon sausage over and sprinkle with the hash brown potatoes. Top with cheddar cheese. Beat the rest together and pour into the crust. Sprinkle with parmesan cheese. Bake at 375° for 25 to 30 minutes.

Coach Dave Odom, Mike Cooke, Jackie Cooke and Billy Canada

Billy Canada

"NOSE," as he is called, was a fraternity brother of mine in the late 1950s and was one of the first members of Carolina Park. He is on the board of directors and is their self appointed spokesman. His "Car Bar" is legendary. He "don't" always throw strikes, but you can always count on him.

Cathead Biscuits
Billy Canada

6 lbs. self-rising flour
1 lb. can shortening, Crisco
½ gal. Buttermilk

Stir together flour, shortening and buttermilk; Roll out to about 1 inch thick; cut large biscuits about 3 inches; Bake on greased baking pan 425° until golden brown.

Cook for about 35 to 40 minutes.

Cheese Biscuits
Mary Hughes

1 lb. cheddar cheese (softened or shredded)
2 1/2 sticks margarine or butter
3 1/2 cups all-purpose flour
1/2 tsp. salt
1/4 tsp. red pepper
2 tsp. baking powder.

Cream together cheddar cheese and margarine (or butter). Sift together flour, salt, red pepper and baking powder. Mix all ingredients. Make into small rolls, wrap in waxed paper and keep in refrigerator overnight or a few hours. Cut into thin slices and bake in 350° oven (on ungreased cookie sheet) until done about 10-15 minutes.

Corn Bread For 120
Zoe & Alex Sanders

When making this corn bread we have always used Adluh self-rising yellow cornmeal, which is made in Columbia.

1 (1 lb.) can Crisco shortening
1 (5 lb.) bag self-rising yellow cornmeal
½ lb self-rising flour
1 tbsp. salt
12 eggs, lightly beaten
½ gal. milk
½ gal. buttermilk

Two (26x18) pans, greased with shortening. Preheat oven to 425° or convection oven to 400°.

Melt shortening and cool. Mix cornmeal, flour, salt, and sugar. Add eggs and mix very lightly by hand until eggs "disappear." Add milk and buttermilk and stir gently. Add melted shortening and gently mix. Do not mix until batter is smooth and a bit lumpy. Lumpy batter makes better corn bread. Pour batter into greased pans and bake in either oven for 15 minutes, or until it starts to brown and begins to pull away from sides of pans.

Breads

Dill Bread
Eddie Elmore & Gene Ransdale

1 stick of butter
2 cans of flaky Biscuits (Grand, Jumbo or Extra Large)
Ground Dill Weed
Dill Seed

Melt Butter and pour in to the bottom of a scalloped bunt pan. Sprinkle dill seed in the melted butter in the bottom of bunt pan. Separate the biscuits and sprinkle ground dill weed over each biscuit. Place the biscuits vertically in the melted butter around the edge of the bunt pan. Sprinkle dill seed on top of the biscuits. Bake in preheated oven @ 400° until biscuits are brown on top. Remove from oven and serve while hot.

Dilly Casserole Bread
Susie & Heyward King

1 pkg. yeast
¼ cup warm water
1 cup cottage cheese, heated to lukewarm
2 tbls. sugar
1 tbl. instant minced onion
1 tbl. butter
2 tsp. dill seed
1 tsp. salt
¼ tsp. soda
1 unbeaten egg
2 ¼ to 2 ½ cups plain flour

Soften yeast in water. Combine cottage cheese, sugar, onion, butter, dill seed, salt, soda, egg, and yeast. Add flour to form stiff dough. Beat well. Cover. Let rise in a warm place until double in size. Turn into a well-greased 8" round casserole. Let rise until light (30-40 minutes). Bake 350° for 40-50 minutes. Brush with butter. Makes 1 round loaf.

Easy Whipping Cream Biscuits
Susie & Heyward King

1 ½ cup self-rising flour, sifted
1 cup heavy cream
½ stick butter, melted

Place flour in bowl, add cream. Stir quickly until ingredients are just moistened. Gently press into 9x12 pan in which you have melted ½ stick of butter. Cut with a knife the size biscuits you want. Do not separate. Brush with melted butter.

Bake at 450° for 12-15 minutes. Break apart.

Hot Water Corn Bread
Keith Wright

1 cup corn meal
½ cup flour
1 tsp. salt
Boiling water
Cooking Oil

Blend dry ingredients. Add boiling water to make a very stiff batter. By using a spoon make small pones and drop in deep hot grease and brown on all sides.

Breads

Johnny Grambling, Blackie Kincaid, Bill Wohrman & Gene Wilson

Brad Edwards

Brad is best remembered for his return interceptions for touchdowns against Clemson in both the 1986 and 1987 games. Brad went on from there to a 10-year NFL career, playing for the Vikings, Redskins, Falcons and Packers. He played in Super Bowl XXVI.

Johnny Grambling

South Carolina's first to surpass 2,000 career passing yards. He played for the Ottawa Roughriders in the Canadian League in 1954, but his professional career was cut short by military service in the Korean War.

Hush Puppies
Brad Edwards

2 cups sifted meal
½ cup sifted flour
½ cup onions (cup up)
2 tsp. baking powder
1 tsp. salt
2 eggs
Buttermilk

Mix the first six ingredients together then add enough buttermilk to make the mix as thick as you like.

New England Corn Fritters
Johnny Grambling

2 eggs, well beaten
1 cup milk
2 cups all-purpose flour
4 tsp. baking powder
¾ tsp. salt
2 cups cream-style corn
¼ cup shortening
½ cup onion, grated, (optional)
Melted butter, syrup, or sugar

Beat eggs with milk, flour, baking powder, salt, corn, shortening, and onion, if desired. Generously grease griddle or frying pan and heat until a drop of batter sizzles. Drop batter by spoonfuls onto griddle or pan. In about 2 minutes, when bubbles appear, turn and brown on other side. Transfer to heated platter. Serve with melted butter and syrup or sugar.

Breads

Ryan Brewer

"Mr. Football" in the State of Ohio, Ryan was one of Lou Holtz's first recruits at Carolina who was a wide receiver, running back, kickoff and punt returner. M.V.P. in the 2001 Outback Bowl. Injuries hampered him in his senior year, but he was an inspirational leader and co-captained the team. He played with his head and his heart and was my favorite player.

Patsy's Strawberry Bread

Ryan Brewer
Submitted by Patsy Wainwright

2 tbsp. cooking oil
12 eggs
1 ½ cups milk
1 tsp. cinnamon
1 tsp. salt
2 tbsp. sugar
18 slices stale bread
1 qt. strawberries, sliced
Powdered sugar

Heat oil in skillet until medium-hot. In a large bowl, mix eggs, milk, cinnamon, salt and sugar until frothy. Dip bread into mixture to cover both sides and fry until brown. Flip bread, smother with strawberries and cook until bread is brown. Top with powdered sugar.

Serve Immediately.

Pumpkin Bread

Margaret & Ruddy Attaberry

1 cup shortening
2 ¾ cups sugar
3 eggs
3 cups flour, plain
1 tsp. baking powder
1 tsp. nutmeg
1 tsp. soda
1/8 tsp. salt
1 tsp. all spice
1 tsp. cinnamon
1 # 303 can pumpkin (2 cups)
1 tsp. vanilla
1 cup pecans, chopped

Cream shortening and sugar, Add eggs one at the time. Add remaining ingredients and beat until well blended. Pour into 2 greased 8 ¼ x 4 ½ x 2 ½ loaf pans. Bake one hour at 350°.

Saute onions in the butter until transparent. Mix Bisquick mix and ½ cup cheese together. Combine egg, milk and onion. Add all at once to Bisquick mixture and beat vigorously for 30 seconds. Fill well greased muffin tins 2/3 full. Sprinkle tops with some of the grated cheese and sesame seeds. Bake at 400 degrees for 12 to 15 minutes.
Servings: 12.

Todd Ellis

Todd was a four-year starter and threw for a school record 9,954 yards from 1986-1989. His 97-yard toss to Robert Brooks was a school record until a 99-yarder from Pinkins to Troy Williamson. Todd threw for 425 yards in one game and is second only to Steve Tanneyhill. Todd spends a lot of time playing golf for charity organizations and is in his fourth year of doing play-by-play on the Gamecock Network.

Sesame Cheese Muffins
Todd Ellis

1 ½ cups Bisquick biscuit mix
¾ cup sharp cheddar cheese, grated
¼ cup onions, minced
1 egg, well beaten
½ cup milk
1 tbsp. sesame seeds, toasted

Chili & Soups

Black-eyed Pea Gumbo - Frank Beatty

Chicken Tortilla Soup - Stuart Whatley

Chili - Bright Stevenson

Guadeloupe - Frank Beatty

Gloulash - Dick Harris

Jambalaya - Melvin Wright

Okra-Oyster Soup - Margaret & Ruddy Attaberry

Puree Mongole Soup - Howard & Sandra Hughes

Taco Soup - Susan and John Moore

Tuscan Vegetable Soup - Hannalie & Red Ferguson

Black-eyed Pea Gumbo
Frank Beatty

1/3 cup vegetable oil
1/3 cup all-purpose flour
2 tbsp. vegetable oil
1½ cups okra, chopped
1 cup onions, chopped
¾ cup celery, chopped
3 cloves garlic, peeled and minced
4 cups water
2 cups tomatoes, chopped
1/3 cup fresh parsley, chopped
1½ tsp. salt
½ tsp. dried thyme
¼ tsp. cayenne pepper
¼ tsp. ground black pepper
2 bay leaves
½ lb. andouille sausage, sliced
½ lb. cooked ham, cubed
1 can (28 oz) black-eyed peas

Heat 1/3 cup oil in a medium saucepan over medium low heat and whisk in flour. Whisking constantly, cook 5 to 7 minutes until brown roux has formed.

Heat 2 tablespoons oil in a large heavy saucepan over medium high heat. Stir in okra, onion, celery and garlic. Cook for 10 minutes or until tender.

Thoroughly blend roux into the vegetable mixture. Stir in water, tomatoes, parsley, salt, thyme, cayenne pepper, black pepper and bay leaves. Bring to a boil, reduce heat and simmer for 20 minutes, stirring occasionally.

Mix in ham and sausage and continue cooking until tender, about 15 minutes. Stir in black-eyed peas and continue cooking until heated through. Serve over rice or in a bowl with cornbread side.

This recipe makes 10-12 servings and tastes even better if allowed to sit overnight, or a couple of nights, before heating and serving.
Smoked turkey can be substituted for the ham.

Chicken Tortilla Soup
Stuart Whatley

1 small onion, chopped
1 fresh jalapeno, deseeded and chopped
2 cloves garlic, minced
2 lbs. shredded chicken
1 16 oz. can of stewed tomatoes
1 10 oz. can of tomatoes with green chilies
1 10 ¾ oz.can of chicken broth
1 10 ¾ oz. can of tomato soup
1 tsp. ground cumin
1 tsp. chili powder
1 tsp. salt
1 tbsp. fresh cilantro
6 corn tortillas cut into ½ inch strips
½ cup of cheddar cheese, grated
2 tbsps. vegetable oil
1 ½ cups water

Fry the tortilla strips in vegetable oil. Drain on paper towel and reserve. Sauté the onions, garlic, jalapeno, chicken in oil. Add tomatoes and other ingredients and bring to a boil. Lower heat and cover for 1 hour to simmer. When done add the tortillas and cheese. When serving suggest top with sour cream, chopped black olives and green onions.

Bright Stevenson

I first met Bright in the fall of 1956. Bright owned the Coronet Motel and the Circus Room Night Club in Eastover. The Circus Room had the finest food and the only mixed drinks in the Columbia area at that time. What Bright does best is cook and he can cook for the masses. By that I mean 1,200 people at one time or 3,000 on a weekend. He helped cater the first Wildlife Expedition in Charleston. Bright says he has retired a little, but you can't prove it by me.

Chili
Bright Stevenson

1 lb. ground beef
1 large onion, chopped
1 green pepper, chopped
2 cloves of garlic, chopped
1 16 oz. can tomatoes
2 medium bay leaves
2 tbsp. chili powder
2 tsp. salt
1/8 cayenne pepper
1/8 tsp. paprika
1 can Chili beans

Brown butter and onion, and green pepper. Add remaining ingredients except beans. Cover and cook (simmer) about two hours or more if you want. Last 1/2 hour add beans.

Guadeloupe Chili Pie
Frank Beatty

2 lbs. ground beef
1 medium onion, chopped
1 can (15 oz) chili beans
1 package (6 oz) cornbread mix
1 can (8 oz) tomato sauce
2 tbls. vegetable oil
½ tsp. chili powder
½ tsp. salt

Brown beef and onion in a large pot. Add beans, chili powder, salt and tomato sauce; cover and cook for 15 minutes on medium heat. Mix corn bread as directed on package. Pour chili mix into baking pan, cover with cornbread mix, cover dish and cook for 20 minutes at 350°. Uncover dish and continue to cook for another 10-15 minutes until cornbread is done.

Goulash
Dick Harris
Submitted by Bob Cochran

3 lbs. beef shoulder
1 tbsp. bacon grease, butter or shortening
1 green pepper, chopped
1 medium onion, chopped
1 clove of garlic finely chopped
1 tsp. salt
Pepper to taste
1 no. 2 1/2 can tomatoes
1 pkg. spaghetti or noodles

Have the beef cut into small pieces and saute in a hot greased frying pan. Add the chopped garlic, onions, green pepper to this and brown a bit, stirring it around. Now add the tomatoes together with two cups of warm water. Cover, cook slowly for two hours. Have the spaghetti or noodles cooked and drained ten minutes before serving add to the meat mixture. Let cook slowly for ten minutes.

Jambalaya
Melvin Wright

In Louisiana cooking, the trio of onion, celery, and bell pepper is called "the Trinity" and it is essential to this dish. Using fresh or canned tomatoes is your call-both work fine.

8 oz. kielbasa, sliced into 1/2 inch thick rounds
2 tbsp. olive oil
2 cups onions, chopped
1 cup celery, chopped
1 cup red bell pepper, chopped
1 lb. medium shrimp, peeled, deveined
2 tsp. garlic, minced
4 cups tomatoes, chopped
2 cups cooked white rice
2 tsp. Tabasco, or to taste
Salt & pepper to taste
Chopped scallions

Brown kielbasa in oil in a saute pan over medium-high heat, about three minutes. Stir in onions, celery, and bell pepper; saute five minutes. Add shrimp and garlic; cook for three minutes more, stirring constantly. Stir in tomatoes and rice; cook 3-4 minutes to heat through. Season with Tabasco, salt, and pepper. Garnish with scallions and serve.

Okra-Oyster Soup
Margaret & Ruddy Attaberry

¼ cup butter or margarine
½ lb. cooked ham, diced
2 cups raw chicken, diced
1 lb. fresh okra, washed and sliced (Or)
2 packages (10 oz. each) frozen okra-thawed
2 cups onions, diced
1 green pepper, diced
1 clove garlic, minced
1 can (1 lb. 12 oz.) tomatoes, chopped
2 cans (13 ¾ oz. each) chicken broth
2 dozen oysters, drained-liquid reserved
½ tsp salt
½ tsp. red pepper

Melt butter in heavy saucepan over medium heat. Add ham, and chicken. Cook 2 minutes stirring frequently. Add okra, onion and green pepper. Cook 5 minutes stirring frequently. Add garlic, tomatoes, chicken broth, and liquid from oysters, salt and red pepper. Bring to boiling, simmer 45 minutes. Add oysters and cook 1 minute. Bakes 8 to 10 servings.

Puree Mongole Soup
Howard & Sandra Hughes

Ironically, not only was this FBI Director, J. Edgar Hoover's favorite soup but it was also quite popular in the White House during President Kennedy's administration. It was invented by Louis Diat, chef at the Ritz-Carlton Hotel in New York City, where he invented that American classic vichyssoise. The hardest thing about this recipe is finding a grocery store that sells cans of condensed green pea soup, Perfect for cold weather feeds.

1 can Campbell's condensed green pea soup
1 can Campbell's condensed tomato soup
1 can evap. milk
1 can water
Dash of curry powder

Mix all ingredients in a blender, Heat and serve.

Taco Soup
Susan & John Moore

1 lb. ground beef, browned and drained
1 can pinto beans, with juice
1 can red kidney beans, with juice
1 can black beans, drained
1 can niblet corn, drained
1 can chicken broth
1 cup onions, chopped
1 pkg. Taco seasonings
1 pkg. Hidden Valley Ranch dressing, dry
1 can mild Rotel tomatoes
1 large can diced tomatoes

Mix all the above, bring to a boil for 10 minutes, and simmer for 30 minutes. Serve with sharp Cheddar cheese, shredded, and Fritos, on top.

Tuscan Vegetable Soup
Hannalie & Red Ferguson

1 1 lb, pkg dried cannelloni (white kidney beans)
2 tbsp. olive oil
1 large onion. chopped finely
2 tbsp. fresh thyme, chopped
4 garlic cloves, minced
1/4 head of cabbage, cut into ½ " pieces
2 cups tomatoes, chopped
4 celery stalks, chopped
3 carrots, chopped
10 cups canned vegetable stock
2 medium potatoes cut into ½ " pieces
½ tbls. fresh basil, chopped
½ head of red cabbage, cut into ½ " pieces
4 zucchini, cut into ½ " pieces
6 slices 7 grain bread, toasted
1 cup Parmesan cheese, grated
Additional olive oil

Cover beans by 3 inches of water, soak overnight. Drain.

Head 2 tbsp olive oil add next 3 ingredients, sauté 5 minutes. Add green cabbage, tomatoes, celery, carrots; sauté 10 minutes. Add beans, 10 cups of stock, potatoes, and basil. Reduce heat and simmer for 1 hour. Add red cabbage and zucchini. Cover and simmer until vegetables are tender, about 20 minutes longer. Uncover, add toasted bread slices to soup and remove from heat. Stir in cheese. Divide soup among bowls. Top with ground pepper and additional olive oil and serve.

Dips & Sauces

Bean Dip - Susan Hughes

Broccoli Dip - Frances Sloan Fulmer

Caramel Apple Dip - Lucy Hughes

Cold Crab Dip - Brenda Cheek

Corn Dip - Betty & Don Barton

Crab Dip - LTC Alfred Johnson USMC (retired)

Hot Crab Dip - Frances Sloan Fulmer

Hot Crab and Cream Cheese Dip - Pam Harrison

Hot Crabmeat Dip - Ginger & Roy McLaurin

Junk Dip - Trish & Warren Norris

Mama Vickers Shrimp Dip - Robbie & Sam Vickers

Pepperoni Pizza Dip - Cheryl & Ken Wheat

Ranch Dip - John Mark Calhoun

Salmon Dip - Cheryl & Ken Wheat

Salsa Fuego - Frank Beatty

Seven Layer Dip - Betsy & Ronnie Collins

Shrimp Dip No. 1 - Ben & Louise Galloway

Shrimp Dip No. 2 - Billy Canada

Shrimp Dip No. 3 - Herbert & Gwen Adams

Shrimp Dip No. 4 - Sheila Fulmer

Spicy Sausage Dip - John Mark Calhoun

Taco Dip - Mary Kay & Chip Wilson

Taco Dip - Sheila Fulmer

Tennessee Dip - Sheila Fulmer

Three-Cheese Dip - Mary & Camden Lewis

Bean Dip
Susan Hughes

1 8-oz. pkg. cream cheese, softened
1 can Hormel Vegetarian Chili and Beans (if can't get
Vegetarian, I use the Turkey Fat Free)
4-6 jalapeno slices (fresh or slices from a jar)
1 pkg. Monterrey Jack cheese, grated
Nacho chips

Spread cream cheese in glass baking dish. Spread
chili and beans on top of cream cheese. Space a few
jalapeno slices around on top of chili and beans (not
many unless you want it really hot). Cover with grated
cheese. Bake either in microwave or regular oven until
hot throughout and cheese is melted completely. Serve
with nacho chips. Can double recipe for larger group.

Broccoli Dip
Frances Sloan Fulmer

1 roll garlic cheese
1 can cream of mushroom soup
1 pkg. frozen broccoli
½ cup celery, chopped
½ cup mushrooms, chopped
½ stick butter
3 tbsp. lemon juice

Sauté chopped mushrooms and celery in butter. Cook
broccoli until very soft, drain and chop; add to sautéed
mushrooms and celery. Stir in soup and cheese. Stir
until cheese melts. Add lemon juice.
Serve with crackers or chips.

Caramel Apple Dip
Lucy Hughes

1 8-oz. bar cream cheese (softened)
1 container Caramel Dip (for apples --
usually found in the produce area)
1/2 bag of Heath Bar Toffee pieces (found in the baking
products aisle near chocolate chips, nuts, coconut, etc.)
Apples (sliced)

Layer cream cheese with caramel dip on top in serving
dish. Sprinkle (amount optional per taste) Heath Bar
Toffee pieces over caramel dip. Slice apples and dip in
mixture. Can serve immediately upon fixing, but keep
refrigerated if made earlier than serving time and refrigerate any leftovers.

Cold Crab Dip
Brenda Cheek

16 oz crab claws
1 cup Duke Mayonnaise (more if desired)
7 tbs. French dressing
½ cups onions, chopped
3 tbs. horseradish, or more to taste
1 ½ cup sharp cheddar cheese, shredded
Salt and pepper to taste
Lemon juice if desired

Combine all ingredients and chill for a couple of hours.

Corn Dip
Betty & Don Barton

2 bags white shoe corn (Green Giant)
8 oz. cream cheese
1 stick butter
1 jar (12 oz.) sliced jalapeño peppers, drained
Garlic salt to taste

Melt cream cheese and butter on low. Add corn and stir to coat corn. Simmer for 15 minutes, stirring often. Add pepper and remove from heat. May prepare a day ahead and refrigerate. When serving, heat in 350° oven until bubbly.

Crab Dip
LTC Alfred Johnson USMC (retired)

3 (8 oz.) cream cheese
1 cup crab meat
2 tbls. mayonnaise
2 tbls. onion, finely chopped
Dash of Worcestershire
Top with paprika

Cook at 350° until brown and puffs, approx. 20-25 minutes. This is my daughter, Jeanne's recipe. It is great!

Hot Crab Dip
Frances Sloan Fulmer

1 can cream of celery soup
1 can cream of asparagus soup
1 stick butter
Sherry
2 6 oz. pkg. frozen Alaska king crab meat (thaw crab in a colander under cold water and break apart chunks of crab. Then squeeze excess water from the crab meat.)

Melt butter in sauce pan. Add both soups then crab meat. Bring slowly to a boil, stirring regularly. Add sherry and stir well to blend in. Serve from a chafing dish with small patty shells.

Hot Crab Dip
Pam Harrison

3 8 oz. cream cheese
3 large cans of crabmeat (or use fresh)
½ cup mayonnaise
1 tsp. grated onion
1 tsp. onion juice
½ tsp. horseradish
1 tsp. Dijon mustard
Dash garlic salt and seasoning salt

Mix all together and heat. Serve with crackers.

Hot Crabmeat Dip
Ginger & Roy McLaurin

1 lb crabmeat,
1 ½ cups mayonnaise
1 cup of grated Swiss cheese
2 bunches of scallions (cut into the green)
1 tbsp. lemon juice.

Mix all ingredients and put in shallow baking dish. Grate some cheddar on top and bake at 350 degrees for 15 or 20 minutes - till hot and bubbly. Serve HOT with crackers.

Dips & Sauces

45

Julia Madison Haunert

We won every game she attended at home in 2005, tailgating at University House.

Dips & Sauces

Junk Dip
Trish & Warren Norris

1 small (4.5 oz.) can black chopped olives
1 small (4.5 oz.) can green chopped chilies
2 large ripe tomatoes chopped
3 to 4 green onions, chopped
1 tsp. garlic salt
3 tbls. olive oil
1 ½ tbls. white vinegar
1 tsp. salt
¼ tsp. pepper

Mix all ingredients and store in a plastic container. Serve with nacho chips.

Mama Vickers Shrimp Dip
Robbie & Sam Vickers

1 8 oz. container sour cream
1 8 oz. package cream cheese
3 tbsp. mayonnaise
1 can tiny shrimp, drained
Hot sauce to taste

Combine all ingredients. Dip potato chips and enjoy!

Place into ceramic quiche plate or suitable container. Bake 350° for 10 minutes. TOP: ¼ cup shredded mozzarella cheese. Bake for 5 minutes more.

Serve with Frito scoop chips or your favorite cracker.

Ranch Dip
John Mark Calhoun

1 pkg. of powder ranch dip or dressing
1 16 oz. pkg. of sour cream
1 cup of finely shredded cheddar cheese
1 bottle of bacon pieces (not bacon bits)
1 bag of ruffled or wavy chips

Add powdered dip, sour cream, cheese and bacon and mix well, and then refrigerate for one hour.

Dip your chips in Ranch Dip.

Salmon Dip
Cheryl & Ken Wheat

1 can Salmon
Mayonnaise to taste
Dill Pickle Chips, chopped to taste
Seasoning Salt
Lemon Juice

Mold Salmon onto a serving plate. Mix remaining ingredients and pour over salmon. Serve with toast points.

Kent Wheat

COCKS CORNER is just one of many, many successful developments engineered under the guidance of Ken's watchful eye. President of Boyd Management, Wheatie rules the roost at Cock's Corner. He and his wife, Cheryl, have three daughters, Kimberly, Leslie and Lori. Ken have always been a very passionate and physical man. He finally got a male grandson, Will, that I have every reason to think will be spoiled rotten.

Pepperoni Pizza Dip
Cheryl & Ken Wheat

8 oz. cream cheese
½ cup sour cream
½ tsp. Italian Seasoning
½ tsp. oregano
1/8 tsp. garlic salt
1/8 tsp. crushed red pepper flakes
Cream until smooth
Add:
1 cup chopped pepperoni
¼ cup chopped green bell peppers
¼ cup chopped green onions

Dips & Sauces

Salsa Fuego
Frank Beatty

1 jar chopped jalapeno peppers
1 small habanero pepper, deseeded and chopped fine
2 medium onions, diced
2 medium tomatoes, diced
1 tsp. salt
½ cup white vinegar
1 tsp. garlic powder
1 tsp. red pepper
1 tsp. chili poweder
1 can chopped green chilies

Combine all ingredients in a pot, cover and simmer over low heat for one hour. Serve warm. Great if allowed to sit overnight before reheating. This is hot, hot, hot!

2 lbs. ground beef
1 medium onion, chopped
1 can (15 oz) chili beans
1 pkg. (6 oz) cornbread mix
1 can (8 oz) tomato sauce
2 tbls. vegetable oil
½ tsp. chili powder
½ tsp. salt

Brown beef and onion in a large pot. Add beans, chili powder, salt and tomato sauce; cover and cook for 15 minutes on medium heat. Mix corn bread as directed on package. Pour chili mix into baking pan, cover with cornbread mix, cover dish and cook for 20 minutes at 350°. Uncover dish and continue to cook for another 10-15 minutes until cornbread is done.

This serves 6 or 7 peoples.

Judy & Dwight Keith

Dwight is a former captain for the University of South Carolina Gamecock football team and a successful business owner for over 30 years before going into full-time ministry.

He came to a saving knowledge of the Lord Christ in 1973 and since that time, God has used him as a teacher and disciple to the body a well as to those in the world. He and his wife of 41 years, Judy, have established Dwight Keith Ministries, Inc. in 1996. He and Judy have three children and eight grandchildren.

Seven Layer Dip
Betsy & Ronnie Collins

1 can (16oz.) refried beans
1 tbsp. taco seasoning mix
1 cup sour cream
1 cup salsa
1 cup shredded lettuce
1 cup shredded Mexican style cheese
½ cup chopped green onions
¼ cup chopped black olives

Dips & Sauces

Mix beans and taco seasoning mix. Spread onto bottom of 9-inch pie plate. Layer remaining ingredients over beans mixture. Cover and refrigerate several hours or until chilled. Serve with tortilla chips or assorted crackers.

Shrimp Dip No. 1
Ben & Louise Galloway

1 small can tiny shrimp
1 cup of sharp cheese, grated
1 cup of mayonnaise
Small amount of spring onion
Worcestershire sauce, to your taste (4 or 5 drops)

Drain shrimp; mix all ingredients together with crumbled shrimp, chill. Better made 6 hours ahead. Serve with crackers.

Shrimp Dip No. 2
Billy Canada

24 oz. soft cream cheese
3 cans cream of shrimp soup

2 cups chopped mushrooms
1 tbls. crushed garlic with juice
1 tbls. horseradish
1 cup chopped and drained water chestnuts
1 or 2 finely chopped onions
16 oz. of small diced cooked shrimp

Drain shrimp; mix all ingredients together with crumbled shrimp, chill. Better made 6 hours ahead. Serve with crackers.

Shrimp Dip No. 3
Herbert & Gwen Adams

1 pint Hellmann's mayonnaise
1 small grated onion (to taste)
1 small can shrimp
1 cup finely grated sharp cheese
4 tbls. lemon juice
Dash of Worcestershire sauce

Drain shrimp and soak overnight in two tablespoons of lemon juice. Drain, and add two more tablespoons of lemon juice mixed with mayonnaise, onion, dash Worcestershire sauce and grated cheese to shrimp.
Servings: 8-10

Shrimp Dip No. 4
Sheila Fulmer

8 oz. cream cheese
2 tbls. mayonnaise
1 tbl. lemon juice
¼ cup finely chopped green bell pepper
A few dashes of Tabasco Sauce
3 cans tiny shrimp, rinse and drain on paper towels

Mix all ingredients together and mold in shape.

Spicey Sausage Dip
John Mark Calhoun

1 pkg. of Jimmy Dean "hot" sausage
1 pkg. of Velveeta "Mild Mexican Cheese"
1 can of Rotel diced tomatoes and green chilies
1 bag of Tostados Scoops (chips)

Cube Velveeta cheese and melt in crock pot. Brown sausage and drain and add to cheese. Add diced tomatoes and green chilies.

Dip your chips in Dip. For a milder dip- you may substitute regular Velveeta. For a hotter dip-use the hot version of the Rotel diced tomatoes and green chilies.

Taco Dip
Mary Kay & Chip Wilson

1 pkg. (1.25 oz.) Taco Seasoning
1 (8 oz.) Cream cheese, room temp.
1 (16 oz.) container of sour cream
1 cup of chopped lettuce, fine
2 Roma tomatoes, seeded and chopped fine
1 (8oz.) pkg. cheddar cheese, shredded
1 (3 oz.) can of sliced olives

Mix together cream cheese, sour cream, taco seasoning. Spread on decorative plate. Sprinkle lettuce, tomatoes, cheese, and then olives. Chill one hour before serving. Serve with your favorite chips.

Taco Dip
Sheila Fulmer

2 cans re-fried beans (spread)
16 oz. sour cream
1 cup mayonnaise
1 pkg. taco seasoning
1 tomato, chopped
1 small can chopped black olives

2 spring green onions, chopped
Sharp cheddar cheese, grated

Layer re-fried beans with the mixture of sour cream, mayonnaise and taco seasoning on top. Then add tomatoes, black olives, onion, and cover with grated cheese.

Tennessee Dip
Sheila Fulmer

2 lbs. ground beef
3 pkgs. Mexican Velveeta
2 cans Rotel tomatoes

Heat tomatoes and cheese, until cheese melts. Brown ground beef. Add the meat to cheese mixture. Keep warm. Serve with chips.

Camden Lewis

Cam quarterbacked the Army team that lost to Roger Staubach's Navy team in 1962. In 1969 Cam joined Paul Dietzel and coached under him for three years while attending law school. Cam is now a practicing attorney in Columbia.

Three-Cheese Dip
Mary & Camden Lewis

½ cup blue cheese crumbled
½ cup sharp cheddar cheese shredded
½ cup cottage cheese
½ cup sour cream
1 ½ tsp. onion, grated
½ tsp. Worcestershire sauce

Combine cheese and leave at room temp. Beat with electric mixer till smooth and creamy. Add rest of ingredients. Beat till fluffy. Chill.

51

Salads

7 Layer Salad - Emily White

Angel Salad - Augusta & King Dixon

BBQ Ranch Dressing - Pat & Humpy Wheeler

Blue Cheese Dressing - Shari McKissick

Chicken Broccoli Salad - Diane & Steve Lipscomb

Cole Slaw with Noodles & Nuts - Billy Canada

Cole Slaw - Dottie & Buddy Nidiffer

Donnette's Salad - Martha Seay

Easy Bean Salad - Judy & Dwight Keith

Fruity Chicken or Tuna Salad - Edith & Art Baker

Green Chili Chipotle Ranch Salad - Stuart Whatley

Hot Chicken Salad - Augusta & King Dixon

Marinated Slaw - Pug Wallace

Marinated Vegetable Salad - Betsy & Jim Day

Oak Road Potato Salad - Frank Beatty

Pat's Tater Salad - Pat & Don Weathers

Pistachio Salad - Peggy & Joe Pinner

Potato Salad - Billy Canada

Rice and Shrimp Salad - Terry Kratofil

Roasted Chicken Salad- Stuart Whatley

Strawberry Romaine Salad - M.R. & Sonny Edwards

Taco Salad - Kerry Kratofil

Tuna & Egg Salad - Howard Hughes

Vermicelli Salad - Kay Dievendorf

Pat's Tater Salad - Todd Ellis

Emily White

Coaches come and coaches go, as do Athletic Directors at the University of South Carolina. The only thing that remains stable in our Athletic Department is Emily White.

Emily was hired by Paul Dietzel in January of 1967. Since her hiring, eight coaches and nine ADs have come and gone. In 1988 she had four bosses in one year: Johnny Gregory (interim) Dick Bestwick, Bob Marcum and King Dixon. She is the one constant and there is a very good reason- she is irreplaceable. Smart and good looking, even tempered and organized she is...well...irreplaceable. I don't know what I would do without her.

7 Layer Salad
Emily White

1 head Lettuce, shredded
1 cup Chopped Green Pepper
1 cup LeSueur Peas (be sure to drain)
1 ½ cup Mayonnaise
1 cup Chopped Celery
1 ½ cup Chopped Onions
2 ½ cup Cheddar Cheese, Grated
2 ½ tbsp. sugar
8 slices crisp, crumbled bacon

In a large bowl, layer vegetables in order given above. Spread mayonnaise over them. Sprinkle sugar, cheese and bacon. Cover tightly with foil and refrigerate at least 4 hours before serving (overnight is fine).

Servings: 4

Angel Salad
Augusta & King Dixon

1 pkg. lime jello – pinch of salt
2 3-oz. cream cheese
6-7 marshmallows, chopped
1 small can crushed pineapple
½ cup chopped pecans
1 pint of cream, whipped

Dissolve jello and salt in one cup boiling water. Add marshmallows and cream cheese, which has been mashed with a fork, then add other ingredients. Chill in refrigerator until firm.
Servings: Makes 13-14 individual molds.

BBQ Ranch Salad
Pat & Henry Wheeler

2 cups cubed cooked chicken
1 15 oz. can of black beans, rinsed and drained
2 ears of fresh corn sliced off the cob or 11 oz. of
    canned corn, drained
1 medium tomato, diced
¼ cup of red onion, diced
¼ cup of Hidden Valley BBQ Ranch Dressing
Mixed greens
1 red bell pepper, diced

Combine all ingredients in a medium bowl. Serve chilled and garnished with red bell pepper.

Blue Cheese Dressing
Shari McKissick

¾ cup Mayonnaise
1/8 tsp. Salt
¼ cup Blue Cheese
1/8 tsp. Garlic powder
¼ cup Milk
1/8 tsp. White pepper
1 tsp. Worcestershire sauce

Combine all ingredients. Yields 1 cup.

H.A. "Humpy" Wheeler

He became president and G.M. of what was then the Charlotte Motor Speedway in 1975. In the past 10 years what is now Lowe's Motor Speedway, has increased its seating capacity from 75,000 seats to 167,000 and is the first superspeedway to host night racing.

In 1995 they went public to become the first publicly traded motor sports company on the New York Stock Exchange. He is just as tough as ever and as controversial.

Chicken Broccoli Salad
Diane & Steve Lipscomb

4 oz. vermicelli
1 cup cooked, diced chicken
1 bunch of fresh broccoli
½ cup chopped pecans
½ cup bottled Italian dressing
Cherry tomatoes, optional

Cook vermicelli according to package directions. Drain. Put into bowl and pour dressing over the noodles. Cut tops off the broccoli, using only the flowerettes. (Just use one stalk of the broccoli, not all of the broccoli that will be in the package.) Run the broccoli under very hot water (boiling), until they turn bright green. Add them to the noodles along with the chicken cubes. Toss all together. Chill until ready to serve.

Just before serving, toss in the pecans and garnish with 3 or 4 cherry tomatoes on each serving.
Servings: 2

Cole Slaw with Noodles & Nuts
Billy Canada

1 cup toasted almonds
1 cup toasted sunflower seeds
1 cup chopped green onions tops and bottoms
1 16oz. package slaw mix
2 pkgs. beef flavored Ramen noodles

Mash noodles up good. Put in bottom of bowl.

Layer: Cabbage mix, onions, almonds, sunflower seed. Mix packets from noodles (2) with 1 cup sugar and 2/3 cup of red wine vinegar.

Pour over top. Do not mix up. Refrigerate 24 hours. Mix well and serve.

Cole Slaw
Dottie & Buddy Nidiffer

1 whole cabbage-Cut in half and slice with knife (thin, long shredded strips)
1 cup of Hellmann's Mayonnaise
4 tbsp. white Vinegar or lemon juice
2 tbsp. white onion, grated
2 tbsp. celery seed
2 tbsp. sugar
Salt and pepper to taste

Mix all of above. If prepared a day ahead, keep cabbage and the remainder separate until about 4 hours prior to serving. Left overs are great the next day.
Serves 10-12

Salads

Donnette's Salad
Martha Seay

1/2 cup red wine vinegar
3/4 cup sugar
1 cup oil
2 cloves garlic, minced
1/2 tsp. salt
1/2 tsp. paprika
1/4 tsp. white pepper
1 head each: Boston, Red Leaf, Romaine
1 cup Monterey Jack shredded
1 pint strawberries, sliced thin
1/2 cup chopped walnuts

Mix dressing mixture; pour over salad, cheese, strawberries and walnuts right before serving. Enjoy! Delicious!

Easy Bean Salad
Judy & Dwight Keith

1 can Black Beans
1 can Red Dark Kidney Beans
1 can Garbanzo
1 can Corn
1 Vidalia onion, chopped
1 can Green Peas
1 bottle of Italian Dressing
Salt, Sugar (Optional)

Better if you make 3-4 hours in advance or overnight.
Serves 12

Fruity Chicken or Tuna Salad
Edith & Art Baker

2 (6oz.) cans tuna, drained   OR
4 chicken breasts (4 cups), cooked, skinned and boned.
1 cup chopped dates or raisins
2/3 cup celery, chopped
1 large apple, peeled, cored and diced (not too mellow)
1 tbsp. minced onion (w/ tuna)
1 tsp. soy sauce
¾ cup of white or red seedless grapes, halved

In large bowl, mix part of ingredients with mayonnaise, sweet pickle relish (juice too). May add honey and lemon yogurt. Then add another portion of ingredients and follow the directions. Refrigerate one hour.

Serve on bed of salad greens or wrap in tortilla.

Salads

Green Chili Chipotle Ranch Salad
Stuart Whatley

1 ½-2 heads iceberg lettuce (shredded)
3 yellow tomatoes (quartered), or use cherry
    tomatoes, halved.
Black olives (whole and pitted) cured
4 large radishes (sliced)
Dressing (recipe follows)
2 green onions (thinly sliced)

Green Chili Ranch Dressing:
  1 cup Ranch dressing (Used Ranch Lite)
  1 (4 oz can) diced green chiles, drained
  2 tbsp. Tabasco Chipotle pepper sauce
  1 tsp. finely chopped cilantro
  1 clove garlic, minced
  Whisk all ingredients together and refrigerate

Pile lettuce in 4 bowls. Top with tomatoes, olives, and radishes. Pour on dressing and top with scallions. Simple and good!

Green Chili Chipotle Ranch Salad
Augusta & King Dixon

1 can mushroom soup
2 cups diced chicken, cooked
1 tbsp. lemon juice
¾ cup mayonnaise
½ sliced almonds
3 tbsp. minced onion
1 cup chopped celery
2 or 3 boiled eggs, chopped
1 medium size bag potato chips, crumbled

Grease a pyrex dish or 7 ramekins. Cover bottom with a layer of crushed chips. In a bowl combine all other ingredients, except potato chips, and pour over the top of the chips. Crumble rest of chips over top of casserole. Bake at 400° for 30 minutes.
Servings: 6-7 generously

Alex, Pug, Carol & Friend

J.C. (Pug) Wallace

"Pug" was the owner and proprietor of Pug's at Five Points from 1981-1995. It was the most popular "Watering Hole" in Columbia for most of those years. How and why is anybody's guess? It certainly wasn't Pug's managerial skills.

Pug was in attendance six days and nights a week. He rarely poured a drink and he never cooked a meal, even though he was a good cook. Pug was too "COOL." He was and is a "dapper" dresser and a handsome man who never even considered marriage.

He kept that bar open for 14 years solely on his infectious smile, charming personality and keen sense of humor. Pug made enough money out of that place to retire three times and in fact four or five of his bartenders did. He is now in the garbage business in Myrtle Beach. Nothing has changed; he is still the same loveable character he has always been.

Marinated Slaw
Margaret Chapman
Sister of Pug Wallace

1 3 lb. head cabbage
1 cup vinegar
1 cup sugar
1 tsp. celery seed
1 tsp. salt
¼ cup chopped onion
¾ cup green pepper
½ cup red pepper
1 tsp. mustard seed

Shred cabbage. Heat vinegar and sugar until sugar dissolves and cools. Add celery seed, salt, onion, green and red pepper and mustard seed. Pour over cabbage and refrigerate.

Marinated Vegetable Salad
Betsy & Jim Day

2 (14 ½ oz.) cans of French style green beans
2 (11 oz.) cans of white shoepeg corn
1 (15 oz.) can of sweet green peas
1 medium size green bell pepper, chopped
7 green onions, chopped
1 (2 oz.) jar diced pimentos, drained

Vinaigrette
    1 cup sugar
    ¾ cup cider vinegar
    ½ cup of vegetable oil
    ½ tsp. salt
    ¼ tsp. pepper

Boil 5 minutes, let cool and pour over salad. Refrigerate/ will keep for up to two weeks.

Oak Road Potato Salad
Frank Beatty
(This recipe comes from an article in the Raleigh News and Observer paper and is attributed to Jean White)

5 lbs. Russet potatoes, peeled and cut into large cubes
1 tbsp. kosher salt
5 large eggs, hard-boiled, peeled and chopped into chunks
2 cups chopped sweet onions (Vidalia works nicely)
1 jar (24-oz) sweet gherkin pickles, drained, chopped and juice reserved
2 cups Miracle Whip
½ cup sugar, maybe a little more
1 tbsp. distilled white vinegar
½ tsp. yellow mustard

Place potatoes in large Dutch oven or soup pot. Cover with water and add salt. Place over low heat and bring to a slow boil. Cook, uncovered, until the potatoes are very soft when tested with a fork. Drain and mash the potatoes. A hand mixer can be used for this function. Stir in the eggs, onions and pickles.

In a large bowl, whisk together the Miracle Whip, sugar, vinegar and mustard. Taste and add either sugar or vinegar to get a sweet-tart flavor. Add the warm potato mixture to the dressing and stir to combine. Best if served warm, but will last in refrigerator up to a week. This recipe makes about 16 servings.

Pat's Tater Salad
Pat & Don Weathers

On the morning or evening before the party, boil 12 medium potatoes in skins and two eggs. Keep in refrigerator overnight. Mix:

2 cups mayonnaise
2 tbsp. vinegar
2 tbsp. sugar
1 tbsp. prepared mustard
1 tsp. salt
½ tsp. black pepper
2 tsp. celery seed
1 tsp. mustard seed
½ tsp. ground mustard
½ tsp. turmeric
1 tsp. chili powder
¼ cup vegetable oil

Blend until smooth with spoon or whisk. Put in covered container and refrigerate overnight or day. To prepare: Toss:

Peeled, cubed potatoes
Small jar pimentos
Cubed boiled eggs

Sprinkle with paprika. Serve within two hours or keep in cooler until ready to serve.

Salads

Charlie, Alex, Peggy & Joe

Joe Pinner

Joe Pinner has been working for WIS-TV since 1963 and still is. He has never been fired and has never had an operation. His mind is still as sharp as a razor, and his wit just as keen.

He has been married to Peggy for 49 years and they have two sons and four grandchildren.

Marinated Slaw
Margaret Chapman
Sister of Pug Wallace

1 box pistachio instant jello
1 box lime jello
2 can crushed pineapple with juice
1 cup coconut
1 cup chopped pecans
Mid size container cool-whip
Half bag miniature marshmallows

Mix together and refrigerate over night.

Potato Salad
Billy Canada

6 cups cooked potatoes
4 hard cooked eggs, chopped
1 cup chopped sweet pickles
12 oz. jar diced pimento, drained
½ cup chopped olives
¼ cup finely chopped onions
1 cup mayonnaise
2 tbsp. sweet pickle juice
½ tsp. celery seed
¼ tsp. paprika
Salt and pepper

Combine potatoes, eggs, pickles, pimento, olives and onion in large bowl. Toss lightly and set aside.

Combine salad dressing, mayo, pickle juice and seasonings, Stir until blended. Add to potatoes, stirring well.

Rice & Shrimp Salad
Terry Kratofil

2 lbs. med. Shrimp-cleaned and de-veined
1 pkg. shrimp seasoning (OLD BAY) I used just about
2 TBSP. of the seasoning
   instead of the whole pkg.
1 cup rice
½ cup chopped onion
½ cup chopped green olives
Black pepper
1 cup mayonnaise

Boil shrimp in water to cover with OLD BAY just until pink. Drain shrimp, but RESERVE the water (I use a slotted spoon to take out the shrimp). Put shrimp on paper towel to drain and cool. Return reserved water to pan and add rice and boil rice according to pkg. until tender. Let the rice cool. Once cool, add onion, olives and pepper to taste to the rice. Stir in the mayonnaise. Add cool, dry shrimp (if shrimp is large they can be cut into pieces). Toss and check seasonings (if it needs a little more Old Bay, I would put it in now. I used the whole pkg. and it was very hot and spicy.)

Can be served on lettuce I usually serve with dinner rolls or biscuits.

Roasted Chicken Salad
Stuart Whatley

7 lb. boneless, skinless chicken breasts
Salt and pepper
½ tsp. Cayenne pepper
1 tbsp. Lavender
1 lemon, juice
3 cloves garlic, minced
2/3 cup almonds, sliced and roasted
1 large onion, chopped
Dressing recipe follows
2 tbsp. parsley, chopped
2 tbsp. chives
2 tbsp. tarragon, chopped

Dressing:
1 cup mayonnaise
¾ cup sour cream
¼ cup extra virgin olive oil
2 tbsp. honey
Salt and Pepper to taste
Mix all the above ingredients.

Preheat oven to 400°. Clean chicken, sprinkle with dry seasoning and lemon. Bake in oven until golden brown about 20 minutes. Let chicken cool and pull into small strips. Add almonds, onions and celery and remain-

ing dressing and herbs. Add chicken mix to previously prepared dressing. Can be served as a sandwich or as a salad.

Strawberry Romaine Salad
Martha Ruth & Sonny Edwards

2 heads Romaine lettuce (or 1 Romaine and 1 of an
    other type of lettuce)
1 pint strawberries, sliced
1 cup Monterey Jack cheese, grated
1/2 cup toasted chopped walnuts or pecans
This amount will serve approximately 15 to 20.

Dressing:
1 cup oil
3/4 cup sugar
1/2 cup red wine vinegar
2 cloves garlic, minced
1/2 tsp. salt
1/2 tsp. paprika

May use a blender or food processor to blend ingredients well. Refrigerate dressing. This amount of dressing will be enough for 3 or 4 recipes of salad. Toss salad with dressing at last minute before serving.

Taco Salad
Terry Kratofil

1 lb. ground round-cooked, drained, cooled and put into
    zip lock bag.
1 head of iceberg lettuce- washed and torn into bite
    size pieces and put into a zip lock bag.
¼ small onion-chopped and put into zip lock bag.
1 can red kidney beans-washed and drained and put
    into zip lock bag.
1 tomato-chopped and put into a zip lock bag.
1 small can of sliced black olives-open can, drain and put

Salads

into zip lock bag.
1 (2cup) bag of shredded cheese-Taco or Mexican Blend
1 large bottle of Italian salad dressing.
1 container of sour cream
1 can of jalapeño peppers.
1 bag tortilla chips.
1 large bowl and serving spoon. (I forgot these once)

Prepare all the ingredients as described above and refrigerate until you are ready to place them into a cooler and head out.

When you are ready to serve decide on how big or small of a salad you want and add ingredients to the bowl. Pour some Italian dressing on the salad (little at a time) until it tastes like you want it.

When it is ready, I put the sour cream, jalapeno peppers, and chips by the salad bowl, so people can add it to their salad if they want. I also serve this salad with corn muffins or cornbread.

Tuna & Egg Salad
Howard Hughes

2 large eggs
Pinch of salt
6 oz. tuna (in spring water)
1/2 tsp. freshly ground black pepper
1 tbsp. minced fresh chives
2 tbsp. mayonnaise (I insist on Duke's)
12 stuffed green olives (chopped)

Place the eggs in a medium saucepan with water to cover and add the salt. Bring to a boil over moderately high heat. Reduce the heat to moderate and boil gently for 10 minutes. Drain and add cold running water to the pot. Let the eggs sit in the cold water until cool. Peel the eggs and finely chop. Place in a medium bowl and toss with the tuna. Stir in the mayonnaise, pepper,

olives, and chives. Season with additional salt to taste (Morton's Hot Salt can really liven it up).

Vermicellie Salad
Kay Dievendorf

1 pkg. vermicelli, cooked
1 (6 ½ oz.) jar marinated artichoke hearts and juice
2 large tomatoes, chopped
1 cup fresh mushrooms, sliced
½ cup walnuts, chopped
¼ cup vegetable oil
¼ cup red wine vinegar
1 large clove garlic, minced
¼ tsp. dried whole basil
Italian dressing to taste
Lettuce leaves

Mix artichoke heart juice with vegetable oil, red wine vinegar, garlic, pepper, salt and basil. Mix cooked vermicelli, tomatoes, mushrooms, artichoke hearts, parsley and walnuts. Mix altogether. Add Italian dressing to taste. Let sit in refrigerator overnight. When ready to serve, put lettuce leaves around salad.

Sandwiches

D.E. Neeley's Bar -B-Q Sauce - Leslie & Roy Hart

Granddaddy Neeley's Chicken Bar-B-Q Sauce - Leslie & Roy Hart

Championship Cheerwine BBQ Sauce - Frank Collins

Quick Welsh Rabbit - Joyce & Bobby Sumwalt

Pimento Cheese Recipe - L.D. (Brother) Pit

Ice-Box Tuna Sandwiches - Dan Reeves

Ham Rolls - Julie & John Saunders

Ham Delights - Doug & Louise Hatcher

Chipped Ham BBQ Sandwiches - Terry Kratofil

Sloppy Joes - Terry Kratofil

Vietnamese Grilled Pork Sandwiches - Liz & Jim Duncan

D.E. Neeley's Bar-B-Que Sauce
Submitted by Roy "Pop" & Leslie Hart

14 oz. Ketchup
5 oz. Worcestershire Sauce
1 tbsp. Black Pepper
1 tsp. Red Pepper
1 cup White Vinegar

Mix all the above ingredients together.

Pop's version of Granddaddy's recipe (above)

36 oz. Ketchup
20 oz. Worcestershire Sauce
56 oz. Prepared Mustard
4 tbsp. Black Pepper
4 tsp. Red Pepper
4 cups Apple Cider Vinegar
4 tbsp. Brown Sugar

Granddaddy Neeley's Chicken Bar-B-Que Sauce
Submitted by Roy "Pop" & Leslie Hart

1 lb. Real Butter
1 qt. & 1 pt. Miracle Whip Salad Dressing
1 pt. (French's) Mustard
8 oz. (Real Lemon) Juice
1 pt. White Vinegar
1 cup Ketchup
Salt & Pepper (to taste)
Garlic Powder (optional)

Mix above together.

NOTE: "I have eaten Pop's Chicken BBQ and it is wonderful."
- Charlie Hawkins

Championship Cheerwine BBQ Sauce
Frank Collins

1 12 oz can Cheerwine soft drink
5 oz. molasses
6 oz. brown sugar
10 oz. BBQ sauce as a base (tomato base)
2 oz. white distilled vinegar
$\frac{1}{4}$ tsp. white pepper
$\frac{1}{4}$ tsp. cayenne pepper
$\frac{1}{4}$ tsp. black pepper
$\frac{1}{4}$ tsp. crushed red pepper
1 oz. liquid smoke

Mix well; bring to a boil while stirring. Cool, transfer to a container and refrigerate. Makes approx. 1/3 gal. Use as a marinade or rub. Enjoy with pork, chicken or beef.

*This BBQ Sauce won 3rd place at the Memphis World Championship BBQ Contest.

Sandwiches

Quick Welsh Rarebit
Joyce & Bobby Sumwalt

2 eggs
1 ½ tbsp. butter
1 tbsp. Worcestershire
½ tsp. dry mustard
1 ½ tsp. salt
¼ tsp. pepper
½ lb. sharp cheese, cut up
¾ cup warm beer

Put first six ingredients in blender. Blend. Add beer gradually. Blend until smooth. Serve warm over toast. Can keep warm in double boiler.

Good Sunday supper in the winter time.

L.D. "Brother" Pitts

When I called Brother and asked for a recipe, picture and short resume here is what I got. I didn't qualify as a jock in college, but I was a large "athletic supporter." Photo from 1957 (All-State Cheerleader 1955-1957-Wofford College." It doesn't qualify as an athletic endeavor, but I did ride "shotgun" with Mr. Joel "Wormy" Wall in 1959 in the last South Carolina horse stealing. It cost $7.50 to bail him out of jail. I was never re-paid either. "Nose" Canada phoned in the Story of the Day to a local radio station and received $10.00. Some things never change.

Pimento Cheese Recipe
L.D. (Brother) Pitts

Pimiento (4 oz.)
N.Y. extra sharp Cracker Barrel Cheddar Cheese (10oz.)
Cream cheese (3oz.)
½ tsp. onion powder
1/8 tsp. cayenne red pepper
Duke's Mayonnaise (aprox. 3 tbsp.)

Grate cheddar cheese, drain pimientos. Mix next four ingredients.

Serve with Captain Wafers. Can be used as sandwich mix.

Dan Reeves

Reeves played quarterback for Marvin Bass at Carolina. He was a running back and player-coach for the Dallas Cowboys and was the head coach of the Denver Broncos, New York Giants and Atlanta Falcons.

Ice-Box Tuna Sandwich
Dan Reeves

These delicious sandwiches assembled a day ahead take only 10 minutes to complete. They are ideal at a brunch.
Filling:
    2 7 oz. can white tuna, drained and flaked
    ½ cup ripe olives, chopped
    ½ cup green bell peppers, chopped
    4 hard-cooked eggs, chopped
    2 tbs. freshly squeezed lemon juice
    2/3 cup mayonnaise
    Salt and freshly ground pepper to taste

Icing:
    8 oz. pkg. cream cheese
    ¼ cup lightly salted butter
    2 eggs, beaten
    ¼ tsp. garlic, minced
    ¼ tsp. basil
    1/8 tsp. salt
    1/8 tsp. freshly ground pepper
    16 slices bread, crusts removed

To make fillings, combine tuna, olives, bell peppers, eggs, lemon juice, mayonnaise, salt and pepper.

To make icing, combine cream cheese with butter, eggs, garlic, basil, salt and pepper. Beat with electric mixer 5 minutes, until fluffy.

Spread one slice of bread with filling and top with second slice. Repeat to make 8 sandwiches. Generously ice sides and tops. Refreigerate. Preheat broiler. Set on baking sheet. Broil 3 to 5 minutes.

Sandwiches

3 tbsp. poppy seed
1 tsp. Worcestershire sauce
1 small onion, grated

Melt margarine and add other ingredients. Next, spread sauce on four-pkg. Pepperidge Farm dinner rolls that have been sliced in two (Spread on both halves). Fill rolls with a thin slice of ham and Swiss cheese. Wrap in foil and heat 15 minutes at 400°.

These are great to take to football games.

John & Julie Sanders

In 1958 John won the Jacobs Blocking Trophy for both the state of South Carolina and the ACC. He made All-ACC and helped lead the conference in rushing. Injuries side lined him for most of the 1959 season and more or less eliminated any chance for a pro football career. John chose instead to sell hammers and nails and turned it into a very lucrative living.

Illness kept him away from attending Carolina games last year, but he'll be back at his west side parking space this fall. **Welcome Back.**

Ham Rolls
Julie & John Saunders

1 lb. baked or boiled ham, sliced thin
5 oz. Swiss cheese
4-pkg. Pepperidge Farm dinner rolls

Make sauce out of the following:
1 stick margarine
3 tbsp. mustard

Doug & Louise Hatcher

Doug was the punter for the Gamecocks in 1958. If Doug had been 10 feet taller we would have gone to the Orange Bowl that year. Why 10 feet taller? Because that's how far over his head Dwight Keith snapped the ball that Doug finally picked up in the end zone and unwisely ran out to the 2-yard line. Four plays later Maryland scored and they beat us 10-6. Doug has forgiven Dwight. Dwight has forgiven Doug. But no one has forgiven Weemie for dropping a touchdown pass later in the 4th quarter of that same game.

Sandwiches

Ham Delights
Patty Grant, courtesy of Doug & Louise Hatcher

1 lb. package ham, chopped fine
6 oz. Swiss cheese, chopped fine
1 stick soft margarine
3 tbsp. mustard
1 tsp. Worcestershire sauce
1 medium onion, chopped fine
3 package roll, (small brown rolls)

Mix ham, cheese, margarine, mustard, Worcestershire sauce and onion together well.

Split rolls and spread mixture on bottom half. Top with other half and wrap in foil. Bake 10 minutes at 400°. Can be frozen then heated when needed.

Enjoy!

Cucumber Sandwiches
Ruth Grantz

Party bread (light or dark) or white sandwich bread
    with crust removed.
Cucumbers
Mayonnaise
Garlic salt

Peel cucumbers. Spread bread with mayonnaise. Place one slice of cucumber on each piece of party bread or on four corners of white bread. Cut white bread into four pieces. Cover all sandwiches with garlic salt.

Refrigerate overnight.

Chipped Ham BBQ Sandwiches
Terry Kratofil

1 lb. chipped ham (Publix chopped ham sliced THIN)
1 bottle chili sauce
½ bottle water
½ cup ginger ale
Hamburger buns

In a sauce pan, break chipped ham apart. (If sliced thin, tear it into pieces.) Add chili sauce to pan and meat. Fill empty chili bottle half full of water. Put on lid, shake and then pour into pan. Once hot, add ginger ale, stir and heat a minute or so longer. Serve on hamburger bun (like a pulled pork sandwich). I serve potato chips and cole slaw with the sandwich.

We live in Jacksonville, Fla. and head up to Columbia for the games on Friday. So the foods I take are the ones I can make at home, transport in a cooler, and then put together at our tailgating spot.
Servings: Makes about 6 sandwiches

Sloppy Joes
Terry Kratofil

2 lbs. lean ground beef
3-4 tbsp. all purpose flour
1 cup prepared French onion soup
Yellow mustard
Load of white bread
1 med. onion, cut into thin rings

In a large skillet, over med-high heat brown beef, and drain. Return ground beef to skillet and sprinkle on the flour. Add onion soup, stir and cook until meat mixture

Sandwiches

is thickened and most liquid is absorbed.
To serve, spread mustard on 2 slices of bread, add meat mixture to one slice, top with an onion ring or two, and top with other slice of bread and enjoy!
Servings: 6   **breath mints are optional

Jim Duncan

He spent 22 years with Campbell Soups and Reynolds Aluminum and returned to Charlotte in 1983 as Executive Vice-President of Marketing with the Charlotte Motor Speedway. He is semi-retired but still very active with NASCAR.

Vietnamese Grilled Pork Sandwiches
Liz & Jim Duncan

For the pickled vegetables:
    1 garlic clove, crushed
    ½ tsp. salt
    ¼ cup rice wine vinegar
    1 tbsp. sugar
    1/3 cup julienned peeled carrot
    ¼ cup julienned peeled daikon radish

For the sandwiches:
    1 lemongrass stalk, chopped (optional)
    2 shallots, chopped
    1 small jalapeno, chopped
    2 tbs. sugar
    1 ½ tbs. fish sauce
    2 tbs. rice wine vinegar
    3 tbs. sesame oil
    12 oz. pork tenderloin, cut into strips 1/8 inch wide
    1 soft baguette
    2 tbs. mayonnaise
    1 tbs. thinly sliced jalapeno rings
    3 tbs. thinly sliced fresh mint
    2/3 cup loosely packed fresh cilantro leaves
    3 tbsp. Vietnamese dipping sauce

For recipe, go to William Sonoma.com/recipe.

Vegetables & Casseroles

Cheese Grits with Rotel Tomatoes - Sam Rigby & Allen Koon

Black Bean Lasagna - Jake Bodkin

Cheese Grits Casserole - Edith & Art Baker

Chicken Cheese Grits - Myrna & Preacher Whitner

Chicken Party Pie - Cheryl & Ken Wheat

Cold Veggie Pizza - Susie & Heyward King

Corn Casserole - Trish & Warren Norris

Country Macaroni & Cheese - Linda & Mike Withrow

Crab Casserole - Ruth Grantz

Creamed Sweet Potatoes with Orange Cups - Margaret & Ruddy Attaberry

Egg & Shrimp Casserole - Betty & Don Barton

Five Cheese Macaroni & Cheese - Frank Beatty

French Green Bean Casserole - Augusta & King Dixon

Fried Corn - R.C. Moore

Hash Brown Potato Breakfast Casserole - Sheila Fulmer

Hot Chicken Casserole - Ruth Grantz

Hot Tomato Grits - Pam & Pete Minaya

Libba's Okra Rice - Jimmy & Ann Hunter

Macaroni & Cheese - George Rogers

Magaret's Macaroni Casserole - Sonny and M.R. Edwards

Mary's and Willie's Baked Beans - Mary & Willie Jeffries

Mom's Chicken Casserole - Beverly & Herman Hill

Pork Chop Casserole - Edith & Art Baker

Potato Casserole - Myrna & Preacher Whitner

Reba's Beans - Peggy & Paul Trussell

Potatoes A' La Anna - Sterling Sharp

Spinach Cottage Cheese Pie - Bill Jones

Squash Casserole - Kathi & Jimmy Mitchell

Squash Pie - Sandra & Howard Hughes

Sweet Potato Scouffle - Linda & Mike Withrow

Vegetable Casserole - Ria & Edwin Floyd

Cookin' with Cocky II

Bring water, milk and salt to a boil. Add grits and cook according to directions until thickened. Sauté green onions and minced garlic in 1 tbs.of butter. Mix thickened grits with 1 stick of butter, cheeses, garlic and onions and drained Rotel. Put in a butter casserole dish and heat in 350 degree oven until bubbly…20 to 30 minutes…you can put some extra cheese on top and put back in the oven for about 5 more minutes.

Sam Rigby & Allen Koon

Sam graduated from USC in 1957. His grandson Allen is a sophomore, scholarship golfer who played varsity golf as a freshman at the University of South Carolina. Sam gives tips and suggestions to all the Bamberg golfers. Allen doesn't pay any attention to Sam. Allen will do well.

Alex & Jake with 1927 Rio

Cheese Grits with Rotel Tomatoes
Allen Koon & Sam Rigsby
Submitted by Lynn Steedman

2 cups water
1 ¼ cups milk
1 tsp salt
1 cup quick grits
1/3 cup green onions sliced
1 clove of garlic minced
1 stick of butter, plus 1 TBLS
4 oz. Velveeta
2 cups grated extra sharp cheddar cheese
1 can Rotel tomatoes and green chiles, drained

Black Bean Lasagna
Jake Bodkin
Submitted by Frank Beatty

9 lasagna noodles (8 oz)
2 15-oz. cans black beans, rinsed and drained
Non-stick cooking spray
½ cup chopped onion
½ cup chopped green sweet pepper
½ cup red or yellow sweet pepper
2 cloves garlic, minced
2 15-oz. cans low-sodium tomato sauce or tomato sauce with seasonings
¼ cup snipped fresh cilantro
1 12-oz. container low-fat cottage cheese

Vegetables & Casseroles

74

1 8-oa. Pkg. of reduced-fat cream cheese
¼ cup light dairy sour cream
Tomato slices (optional garnish)
Fresh cilantro leaves (optional garnish)

Cook noodles according to package directions; drain. Mash one can of black bean; set aside.

Lightly coat large skillet with cooking spray; add onion, both peppers and garlic. Cook and stir over medium heat until tender but not brown. Add mashed beans, unmashed beans, tomato sauce and snipped cilantro; heat through.

In a large bowl, combine cottage cheese, cream cheese and sour cream; set aside. Spray a 3-quart rectangular baking dish with non-stick coating. Arrange three of the noodles in the bottom of the dish. Top with 1/3 of the bean mixture. Spread 1/3 of the cheese mixture on top of bean mixture. Repeat layers twice, ending with final bean mixture layer and reserve the remaining cheese mixture.

Preheat oven to 350° and bake, covered, for 45 minutes or until heated through. Dollop with reserved cheese mixture and let stand for 10 minutes. Garnish with tomato slices and cilantro, if desired.

Dish can be made ahead and frozen for one month or refrigerated for a couple of days. Recipe makes about 8 servings.

Cheese Grits Casserole
Edith & Art Baker

4 cups water
1 tsp. salt
1 cup grits
6 oz. 1 ½ cups) shredded sharp cheddar cheese
½ cup butter or margarine
1 cup milk
4 eggs, beaten
1/3 tsp. pepper

In large saucepan cook the grits. Remove from heat and add one cup of the cheese and butter; stir until melted. Add milk, eggs and pepper; mix well. Pour mixture into greased casserole. Sprinkle with remaining ½ cup cheese. Bake at 350° for 1 hour or until golden brown. Let stand 10 minutes before serving.

One lb. drained, cooked sausage may be added with milk and eggs.

Chicken Party Pie
Cheryl & Ken Wheat

CHEESE CRUST:
1 cup grated cheddar cheese (at room temperature)
½ cup soft butter
¼ tsp. mustard
¾ cup flour (may need 1 tbsp. more)

Combine cheese and butter. Add mustard and flour. Blend with hands. Form a ball. Let set for a few minutes. Press over sides so shrinkage will be reduced. Prick. Bake at 475° for about 10 minutes.

Vegetables & Casseroles

CHICKEN FILLING:
- 2/3 cup grated cheddar cheese
- 2 cups diced cooked chicken
- I cup chopped nuts
- I cup chopped celery
- ½ cup seedless grapes

Combine I cup sour cream and 2/3 cup mayonnaise. Mix and add 2/3 to chicken filling above. Spread remaining on top. Combine and mix with 2/3 cup of sour cream mixture. Put into baked shell. Spread top with remaining spread. Garnish with olives and cheese. Refrigerate until serving time.

(Given to me by Ellen Turner in 1985)

Cold Veggie Pizza
Susie & Heyward King

- 2 cans crescent rolls
- I (8 oz.) pkg. cream cheese
- ¾ cup mayonnaise
- I pkg. Ranch Dressing mix
- 2 cups finely chopped veggies (broccoli, red pepper, yellow or green, cucumber-your choice or all).

Spread crescent rolls in a large jelly roll pan, sealing seams. Bake at 375° for 10 minutes. Cool. Mix cream cheese, mayonnaise, Ranch dressing pkg. Spread over baked and cooked crescent. Cover with veggies and press in slightly. Top with black olives, sliced cherry tomatoes and shredded cheese. May add green onion if desired. Cover with wax paper and chill 4-10 hours. When ready to serve slice in squares to desired size.

Corn Casserole
Trish & Warren Norris

- I can whole-kernel corn, drained lightly
- I can cream-style corn
- I box Jiffy Cornbread Mix
- I stick margarine
- I cup sour cream
- 2 eggs

Mix all ingredients together and bake 30 minutes at 375°. Remove from oven and top with shredded cheese, return to oven and bake 10 more minutes. This is very good and you will need to make two or three because tailgaters will be coming back for more. Once it is taken from the oven, cover with foil and put in an insulated container until ready for tailgating.

Country Macaroni & Cheese
Linda & Mike Withrow

Elbow Macaroni
Butter
4 eggs
Cheese, such as Pepper Jack, Mozzarella, Sharp Cheddar, Parmesan, Swiss & etc.
Salt and Pepper

Vegetables & Casseroles

Boil elbow macaroni with a little butter and salt (judge amount to cook with number of people serving).

In separate bowl beat 4 eggs slightly. Cut up cheese in small chunks-use any type of cheese desired. Use lots of sharp cheddar for more flavors. Combining several different types of cheese makes delicious touch.

Layer your baking dish with mixture of cheeses first across the bottom of the dish. Then layer macaroni noodles on this. Continue this process until dish is filled (sometimes two to three layers depending on the size of your dish).

Pour scrabbled eggs mixed with salt and lot of pepper over the top of layers. Then pour milk over the top of this until it covers as much of the layers as possible. Layer the very top with sharp shredded cheddar cheese.

Bake in the oven for 20 minutes at 400° then turn oven down to 350° and bake an additional 30 minutes or until top is browned and the center seems firm. Since oven temperatures differ, you will need to carefully watch this for the first couple of times to determine your accuracy with temperatures.

Crab Casserole
Ruth Grantz

Use 3 qt. casserole dish.
1 lb. crab meat
2 cans cream of celery soup
2 cups milk
2 cups uncooked shell macaroni
2 cups shredded cheddar cheese
4 tbsp. grated onion
4 tsp. Old Bay Seafood Seasoning
¼ cup white wine

Combine all ingredients. Place in a slightly buttered casserole. Prepare 1 day ahead. Bake 350° for 45 -60 minutes.

Creamed Sweet Potatoes with Orage Cups
Margaret & Ruddy Attaberry

6 large sweet potatoes, boiled
1 cup sugar
2 eggs, well beaten
½ cups raisins
½ cup milk
1/3 cup butter, melted
Pinch of salt
1/3 cup pecans, chopped
8 oranges

Peel cooked potatoes, cream until smooth. Add sugar, eggs, raisins, milk, butter and salt. Cut oranges in half and remove fruit. Fill orange halves with potato filling. Cook for 20 minutes in a 350° oven. Sprinkle nuts on top. Serve hot.

Eggs and Shrimp Casserole
Betty & Don Barton

8 hard boiled eggs
Mash yolks with:
1/3 cup mayonnaise
½ tbsp. salt
½ tbsp. curry
½ tbsp. paprika
Put in egg whites.

In heavy pot on low heat:
2 cans cream of shrimp soup
½ cup sharp grated cheese
½ lb. of shrimp cooked and cleaned (or more)

Vegetables & Casseroles

77

Arrange eggs in flat casserole. Cover with sauce. Sprinkle with buttered bread crumbs and parmesan cheese. Bake at 350° for 10-15 minutes.

Five Cheese Macaroni and Cheese
Frank Beatty
(This came from Bogart's American Grill in Raleigh, N.C.)

1 qt. heavy cream
8 oz. Swiss cheese, shredded
8 oz. Gouda cheese, shredded
8 oz. Parmesan cheese, shredded
8 oz. Gorgonzola cheese, crumbled
1 box (2 lbs.) macaroni noodles, cooked according to
    pkg. directions and drained

Set rack in top third of overn and preheat broiler.

Bring cream to boil in a large, heavy-bottomed saucepan with an ovenproof handle, taking care not to let the cream boil over. Reduce to a simmer and gradually whisk in the Swiss, Gouda, Cheddar, Parmesan and Gorgonzola cheeses. Continue to whisk until the cheeses are melted and the sauce is thick.

Fold in the well-drained macaroni noodles. Place pan under boiler and heat until the cheese is lightly browned on top, probably 3 minutes or less. Watch constantly as this happens quickly. Serve Warm. This recipe makes 6-8 servings.

Augusta, King III, King II Dixon

While at Carolina, King was an honor student, Phi Beta Kappa. He was VP of the freshman, sophomore and junior classes. He graduated cum laude in 1959.

After college he spent 22 years in the Marines where he was awarded a Bronze and Silver Star. After service, King returned to Laurens and was VP of the local bank.

In 1987 King was named Athletic Director and served in that capacity for six years. He then returned to his bank job in Laurens. King is, of course, a member of the school and state Hall of Fame.

French Green Bean Casserole
Augusta & King Dixon

¾ cup milk
1/8 tsp. pepper
1 can cream of mushroom soup (10 ¾ oz.)
2 cans French Green Beans, drained (14.5 oz.)
1 1/3 cups French's French Fried Onions
Package of sliced almonds
½ cup grated sharp cheese

Vegetables & Casseroles

In 1 ½ qt. casserole put 2 cans of French Green Beans, drained. In a bowl mix all other ingredients except 2/3 cup French Fried Onions. Pour mixture over beans.

Bake at 350 degrees for 30 minutes. Stir. Top with 2/3 cup French Fried Onions, a little grated cheese and (optional) a sprinkling of Pepperidge Farm Corn Bread Stuffing mix. Bake 5 minutes or until onions are golden and cheese is melted.
Servings: 6 - 8

Fried Corn
R.C. Moore
Submitted by Stuart Whatley

4-5 ears of White or Yellow corn
1 lb. bacon
1 large Vidalia Onion
1-2 large Jalapenos
Salt and Pepper

Fry up bacon in deep frying pan until very, very crispy. Remove bacon and drain. Leave about 3 to 5 tbsp. of bacon grease in frying pan (or to your liking). Remove corn from cob and toss corn in hot bacon grease. Add chopped onion and diced jalapeno (deseeded) to the pan.

Cook on medium-high until slightly burned. The onions and corn will start to carmelize. Salt and pepper to taste. Crumble bacon over corn and serve.

Hash Brown Potato Breakfast Casserole
Sheila Fulmer

1 can cream of chicken soup
1 chopped onion
Bell pepper, to taste
1 chopped hot pepper, opt.
30 oz. frozen (thawed) shredded hash browns
8 oz. sour cream
8 oz French onion dip
8 oz. shredded sharp cheese (save some for top)
1 lb. hot sausage

Cook sausage, drain and set aside.
Mix all of the other ingredients.

Spray Pam non-stick cooking spray in bottom of 9x13 dish. Layer ½ mixture, sausage and another layer of sausage and mixture. Sprinkle cheese on top. Bake at 350° for 1 hour.

Hot Chicken Casserole
Ruth Grantz

4 cups cooked diced chicken breasts
2 cups celery, chopped
2 tbsp. onion
¾ cup mayonnaise
1 small jar pimento
1 tsp. salt
1-2 tbsp. lemon juice
1 can cream chicken soup (undiluted)
1 can sliced water chestnuts
1 ½ cups potato chip
2/3 cup slivered almonds

Toss chicken, celery and onion together. Mix with all the other ingredients except potato chips and almonds. Put the mixture in a 9x13 casserole. On top of the casserole add chips and almonds.

Bake 400° for 20-25 minutes.

Hot Tomato Grits
Pan & Pete Minaya

2 bacon slices, chopped
1 (14 ½ oz.) can chicken broth
½ tsp. salt
1 cup quick-cooking grits
2 large tomatoes, peeled and chopped
2 tbsp. canned chopped green chilies
1 cup (4oz.) shredded Cheddar cheese

Cook bacon in a heavy saucepan until crisp reserving drippings in pan. Gradually add broth and salt; bring to a boil.

Stir in grits, (I let simmer for about 10 minutes) and add tomato, and chilies; return to a boil, stirring often.

Reduce heat, and simmer, stirring often, 15 to 20 minutes. Stir in cheese; cover and let stand 5 minutes or until cheese melts. Garnish, if desired, with chopped tomato, cooked and crumbled bacon, and shredded cheddar cheese.

Jimmy Hunter

A native of South Carolina, Jimmy earned three football and two baseball letters at Carolina. In 1993 Jimmy was president of Darlington Raceway. In 1995 Jimmy was awarded the Order of the Palmetto, South Carolina's highest civic honor and was named South Carolina's Tourism Ambassador of the year. Jimmy is currently VP of Corporate Communications for NASCAR.

Libba's Okra Rice
Jimmy & Ann Hunter

4 to 6 slices bacon
1 onion chopped
2 to 3 cups sliced okra
3 ½ cups cooked rice
Salt and pepper to taste

Fry bacon and remove from pan. Sauté onion and okra in drippings. Combine okra and rice and cook in a greased casserole. Bake, covered, 20 to 30 minutes at 325°. You may vary amounts of rice and okra.

Margaret's Macaroni Casserole
Sonny & Martha Ruth Edwards

8-oz. pkg. macaroni, cooked and drained
1 lb. sharp cheese, grated
1 can mushroom soup, diluted with 1 cup milk
1 cup mayonnaise
1 small jar pimentos
1/2 cup chopped onion
1 small can chopped mushrooms
1/2 stick margarine
15 or more crushed Ritz crackers

Cook macaroni without salt and drain. Butter casserole dish. Combine soup, mayonnaise, milk, pimento, mushrooms and onion. Put macaroni in dish; cover with cheese. Spread on soup mixture and cover with crackers.

Pour melted margarine over and sprinkle with paprika and dried parsley. Bake 30 minutes at 300°.

George Rogers and Ben Long

Macaroni & Cheese
George Rogers

George says this is the way his mama makes it.

1 cup, cooked noodles
1 ½ cup milk
1 or 2 eggs
1 (12oz.) cup Sharp Cheese
4 oz. cut up Velveeta cheese
½ cup Parmesan
½ stick butter

Mix and bake at 350° for about an hour.

Mary & Willie Jeffries

Mary and Willie Jeffries are both South Carolinians; Lancaster and Union, respectively. Married for 45 years, Mary has been with Willie through coaching stints in Lancaster, Gaffney (High School), North Carolina A & T, University of Pittsburgh, S. C. State University, Wichita State University, and Howard University. Willie served one year as Athletics Director at Grambling State University in Louisiana.

Willie Jeffries is a legend and I do not use that term loosely or often. I have never met a man who didn't like and respect him. I've known Willie for years, but I've gotten to know him better since I moved to Denmark, S.C. It has been my gain.

I have been to hundreds of banquets all over this country and Willie is the best Master of Ceremony I have ever heard. He alone is worth the price of admission.

Mary's & Willie's Baked Beans
Mary and Willie Jeffries

3 28 oz. cans of Baked Beans or Pork and Beans
½ cup Kraft's Hickory Smoked Barbecue Sauce
¼ cup Kraft's Mesquite Smoked Barbecue Sauce
1 Green Bell Pepper, chopped
1 cup of Packed Dark Brown Sugar
½ lb. Bacon
2 tbsp. of Syrup

Drain beans in a colander. Fry bacon on medium heat, save drippings. Sauté onions and bell pepper in bacon drippings. Add barbecue sauce, brown sugar, syrup and bacon. Reduce heat and simmer for 15 minutes. Add beans and simmer for another 15 minutes.

Mom's Chicken Casserole
Beverly & Herman Hill

2- 3lb. fryers
1 cup water-or more
1 cup Sherry
½ tsp. curry powder
1 onion, sliced
½ cup celery
2 – 6 oz. boxes Uncle Ben's wild rice
1 lb. fresh mushrooms
1 stick butter
1 cup sour cream
1 can cream of mushroom soup

Combine and simmer 1st six ingredients 1 hour. Remove chicken and save liquid. Cook rice with liquid while deboning chicken. Slice and sauté mushrooms in 1 stick of butter. Mix together chicken, rice, mushrooms with sour cream and soup. Pour in casserole dish; cook 30 minutes at 350° oven.

Pork Chop Casserole
Edith & Art Baker

4 pork chops
½ stick margarine
1 medium onion, diced
2 cups beef bouillon or broth
1 cup white rice
Salt and pepper

Season chops and brown quickly. Melt margarine in casserole dish. Add onion and liquids, then rice. Place chops on top of rice.

Bake at 350° for 1 hour (uncovered).

Potato Casserole
Myrna & Preacher Whitner

Red potatoes. Unpeeled
Onions, chopped
Green peppers, chopped
Salt and pepper
Butter

Preheat oven to 350°. 2 qt. DEEP Casserole dish, spray

dish with non-stick spray. Spread a layer of thinly sliced red potatoes (unpeeled). Cover with a layer of chopped onions and chopped green peppers. Salt and pepper and dots of butter across the top.

Repeat layers, ending near the top of the dish with a layer of potatoes. Cover completely and seal edges with cream of mushroom soup.
Bake approximately one hour.

Pork Chop Casserole
Edith & Art Baker

5 slices of bacon
Medium onion
1 lb. ground beef
28 oz. can of pork and beans
16 oz. can of stewed tomatoes
¼ cup of your favorite barbeque sauce
3 tbsp. packed brown sugar
2 tbsp. spicy brown mustard
1 tbsp. red pepper sauce

Fry bacon in a deep 10-inch skillet until crisp. Set bacon aside on paper towels. Drain off grease in skillet. Chop onion and brown in same skillet over medium-high heat for about 5 or 6 minutes. Add ground beef and cook until browned. Drain off excess grease. Stir in pork and beans and stewed tomatoes and barbeque sauce. Next add brown sugar, spicy brown mustard and red pepper sauce.

Reduce heat to medium-low and simmer 15 to 20 minutes. Crumble bacon over top before serving.

Special Instructions: I make this ahead of time and carry in an insulated container. But you could also make at the ballgame.

Sterling Sharp

Sterling was USC's all-time pass receiving leader with 169 career catches for 2,497 yards and 17 touchdowns. He is the top single-season receiver with 74 catches for 1,166 yards and 10 touchdowns that came in 1986. His 104-yard kickoff return is the longest in school's history. Two-time All American, Sterling was an All-Pro player for seven years with the Green Bay Packers.

Potatoes A'La Anna
Sterling Sharp

Potatoes, sliced thin
Butter
Salt and pepper

Take raw potatoes and slice them very thin. Let soak in cold water for three or four hours. Then take them out and dry in a clean towel. Use a glass pie plate for baking. Put one layer of potatoes in the dish; dot the top thickly with butter, also seasoning (salt and pepper). Repeat this until the dish is filled. Bake in moderate oven until well done and nice brown on top. This is delicious served with steak.

Bill Jones in hat

Bill was a fraternity brother and the head-cheerleader for the Gamecocks from 1957-1960. He was also a long distance runner on the track team and a long distance swimmer.

Bill, Mr. Consistency, finished dead last in every event he ever participated in during his four years at Carolina. But he never quit a race…never.
Being a cheerleader back then wasn't easy. Bill said that the largest and loudest noise that came from the USC Stadium was a loud "moan" for the poor fan who had just dropped and broken his bourbon bottle on the concrete floor of the stadium.

Spinach Cottage Cheese Pie
Bill Jones

½ cup onion, chopped
2 tbs. lightly salted butter
2 ten-oz. pkg. frozen chopped spinach, thawed
1 lb. cottage cheese
¼ lb. shredded mozzarella, Muenster, or Swiss cheese
4 eggs
1 tsp. dried dill
Salt and freshly ground pepper, to taste

Preheat oven to 350°. Lightly grease 9-inch deep-dish pie pan. Sauté onion in butter 3 to 5 minutes, until translucent. Add spinach and cook 5 minutes longer, until liquid has evaporated. Combine cottage cheese, shredded cheese, eggs, dill, salt, and pepper. Stir onion and spinach mixture into cheese mixture; blend well. Pour into prepared pan.

Bake 35 to 45 minutes, or until pie tests done.

Squash Casserole
Kathi & Jimmy Mitchell

½ cup seasoned bread crumbs
2 cups squash, cooked and drained
1 cup sharp cheddar cheese, grated
3 tsp. butter, melted
2 tsp. parsley
½ cup onion, chopped
2 eggs, beaten
½ cup half and half

Mix all ingredients. Pour into a buttered casserole dish.

Bake at 350° for 30 to 40 minutes.

Squash Pie
Sandra & Howard Hughes

1 cup grated squash (yellow, no seeds)
1 1/4 cups sugar
3 eggs
pinch of salt
1/2 stick butter or margarine (melted)
2 tbsp. flour
2 tsp. lemon flavoring
2 tsp. coconut flavoring

1/2 cup coconut (optional)
1 deep-dish pie crust

Mix all ingredients together; pour into unbaked pie crust. Bake at 350° for 30 minutes until brown or when knife comes out clean.

Sweet Potate Scouffle
Linda & Mike Withrow

1 2 lb. can of Sweet Potatoes-
   Boil on stove until tender
1 ½ cup sugar
2 eggs
6 tbsp. margarine melted
½ cup milk
½ tsp. cinnamon
½ tsp. nutmeg

Drain potatoes and pour in a bowl. Use your mixer to get a smooth consistency. Add remaining ingredients and heat together (like mush). Pour into a greased 2 quart casserole dish.

Bake at 375° for 20 minutes. Remove from oven and add topping mixture below and bake an additional 15 minutes.

Topping:
   ¾ cups of corn flake crumbs
      (crush corn fakes thoroughly)
   ½ cup chopped pecans (chopped fine)
   6 tbsp. melted butter
   ½ cup brown sugar

Stir topping mixture together and spread over the top of soufflé mixture. Remember bake an additional 15 minutes after spreading the topping.

Vegetables & Casseroles

Vegetable Casserole
Ria & Edwin Floyd

I can white corn, drained
I can french style green beans
I can cream of celery soup
½ cup onion
½ cup bell pepper
I cup sharp cheese
8 oz. sour cream
½ can water chestnuts

Combine all ingredients. Salt and pepper to taste. Top with ½ stick of butter, melted, and one roll of Ritz crackers or ½ box of cheese crackers, crushed. Bake at 350° for 30 minutes.

This is a good dish to take to covered dish affairs. You never have any left over.

Vegetables & Casseroles

Meats

Beaten & Battered Gator - Richard Price

Carolina Pork Barbeque - Sidney Portee

Chicken Carboara - Carman & Bob Clary

Chicken on Fire - Frank Collins

Chicken Parmigiana - Kathi & Jimmy Mitchell

Chicken Piccata - Patsy & John Carroll

Chicken Rice Bog - Billy Canada

Chicken with Big Easy Sauce - Mary Ella Wright

Chipotle Peppered Steak - Frank Collins

Chipotle Rubbed Steaks with Gorgonzola Toast - Stuart Whatley

Cilantro Chili Chicken - Stuart Whatley

Crown Roast of Pork with Cranberry Dressing - Zoe & Alex Sanders

Cuban Dish - Margaret & Ruddy Attaberry

Enchilada Pie - Frank Beatty

Gamecock Vinegar Pepper Pulled BBQ - Lisa & Eddy Richmond

Hamburger Pie - Susie & Heyward King

Hungarian Beef Stew - Hannalie & Red Ferguson

Italian Chicken Stew - Pam & Pete Minaya

Italian Sausage with Peppers & Onions - Tony Soprano & Mike Dana

Kathi's "Killer" Meatloaf - Kathi & Jimmy Mitchell

Marinated Flank Steak - Trish & Warren Norris

Marinated Pork Roast - Mary Ella Wright

Mary Lou's Pot Roast - Pam & Pete Minaya

Mom's Chicken - Beverly & Herman Hill

College of Charleston "Mystery Meat" - Zoe & Alex Sanders

Nide's Duck Tetrazzini - Dottie & Buddy Nidiffer

Northshore Jambalaya - Frank Beatty

Pork Tenderloins with Orange Sauce - Connie and Stan Smith

Roasted Chicken with Balsamic Vinaigrette - Stuart Whatley

Rosemary Lamb Chops - Kathi & Jimmy Mitchell

Savory Baked Pork Chops - Elizabeth & Bill Jerry

Stu's Butt Roast - Stuart Whatley

USC Chicken Spead - Eddy Richmond

Richard Price

Richard Price and his tailgating buddies (Ray Ocheltree, Kevin Barber, Rogers Cannon and Tucker Clifford) have been cooking Beaten and Battered Gator every time the Florida Gators play the Gamecocks in Williams-Brice Stadium. It's always good but it was especially tasty in 2005 when Coach Steve Spurrier's Gamecocks triumphed over the Gainesville Gators.

Beaten & Battered Gator
Richard Price

2 lbs. alligator meat
1 qt. buttermilk
Fish breading (your choice). We use Zatarains Fish Fry
Peanut oil
Salt and pepper

Cut alligator meat into two-inch squares. Soak meat in buttermilk for 24 hours (refrigerated). Heat peanut oil to 350°. Dredge meat in fish breading. Cook in oil until done (golden brown), approximately seven to eight minutes. Drain off excess oil on paper towels. Serve warm. ENJOY! GO COCKS!

Carolina Pork Barbeque
Sidney Portee

4-5 lbs. boneless pork shoulder, Boston Butt
1 qt. cider vinegar
1 to 1 ½ oz. crushed pepper
1 tbsp. black pepper

Stir together vinegar and peppers. Prepare medium-hot coals in covered grill, banking coals when hot. Position drip pan in center of grill bed, between banks of coals. Place pork on grill over drip pan, close hood. Cook for 2 ½ to 3 ½ hours, basting frequently with vinegar marinade until pork is very tender. Remove pork from grill, cool slightly; chop meat and serve with hush puppies and coleslaw, if desired.
Servings: Makes 2 to 3 lbs. of barbecue

Chicken Carboara
Carmon & Bob Clary

1 tbsp. olive oil
4 boneless, skinless chicken breast
1 small onion, chopped
2 slices bacon, chopped
1/3 cup chicken broth
1 jar Alfredo sauce

In 12 inch skillet, heat oil over medium high heat and brown chicken. Remove chicken and set aside.

In same skillet cook onion and bacon, stirring occasionally, 6 minutes or until bacon is cooked. Add broth and cook 1 minute. Stir in Alfredo sauce. Bring to boil over high heat. Reduce heat to low, and then return chicken to skillet. Simmer covered 5 minutes or until chicken is thoroughly cooked.

Meats

Chicken on Fire
Frank Collins

2 small chickens quartered
Salt & pepper
1 cup olive oil
1 tbsp. herbs de Provence
10 cloves garlic, 4 minced, 6 sliced
1 cup cured black olives
Juice of 1 lemon
1 cup Spanish olives
1 lemon, halved and thinly sliced
4 sage leaves
¾ cup cognac

Marinate the chicken in dressing of olive oil, lemon juice, minced garlic, cognac, salt, pepper, sliced garlic, olives and bay leaves. Refrigerate overnight, turning several times. Drain chicken, save marinade in a saucepan. Grill and baste chicken with a little marinade. Heat marinade and pour over chicken to serve.

Chicken Parmigiana
Kathi & Jimmy Mitchell

4 chicken breast halves, boneless, skinless
2 eggs, beaten
1 cup Progresso Italian style bread crumbs
¼ cup olive oil
1 jar Italian Marinara Sauce
½ cup Parmesan cheese, grated
1 cup Mozzarella cheese, shredded

Preheat oven to 400°. Dip chicken in egg and then in bread crumbs. Coat thoroughly. In medium skillet heat oil. Cook chicken in oil until browned on both sides, about 4 minutes per side. Pour sauce into an 11x7 inch baking dish. Place chicken on sauce and top with

cheese. Bake for 15 minutes or until cheese is melted and lightly browned.
Makes 4 servings

Chicken Piccata
Patsy & John Carroll

2 chicken breasts
¼ cup all-purpose flour
¼ tsp. salt
½ tsp. pepper
2 tbsp. peanut or vegetable oil
1/3 cup chardonnay
2 tbsp. butter
2 tbsp. lemon juice
¼ cup chopped fresh parsley
2-3 tbsp. capers
Optional: 1 cup quartered artichoke hearts

Place chicken breasts between wax paper and flatten to 1/8 in. thickness. Cut flattened chicken into 4 pieces. Combine flour, salt, and pepper and dredge chicken through flour mixture. Cook in oil in a skillet over med. heat until browned. Remove from skillet; keep warm. Add wine to hot skillet and cook over high heat. Deglaze by scraping bits that cling to the bottom. Add butter, lemon juice, parsley, peppercorns and artichoke hearts. Add warm chicken to sauce and heat thoroughly.

Serve with angel hair pasta and salad.
Serves 4

Meats

Chicken Rice Bog
Billy Canada

4-6 skinless Breast of Chickens
4-6 thighs
Salt and pepper
Butter
4-5 medium onions, cut up
2-3 stalks celery, cut up
2 cans Cream of Chicken Soup, mixed with water
2 tbsp. mayonnaise
3-4 cups Cheddar Cheese
3-4 cups Rice

Boil chicken pieces in 6-8 cups of water with salt, pepper and butter. Remove chicken when tender. Pull chicken from bones. No skin.

Cook onions and celery in chicken broth until tender and add soup mix and mayonnaise. Use 6-8 cups of broth. Add chicken and bring to a boil. Reduce to low heat and add 3-4 cups rice, cover and cook 20 to 30 minutes. When the rice is done, fluff the rice and add 3-4 cups of shredded cheddar cheese. Mix in well.

Chicken with Big East Sauce
Mary Ellen Wright

4-6 oz. boneless chicken breast
Cajun seasoning
6 oz. andouille sausage
6 oz. crawfish tails
1 tbsp. chopped green onions
1 tbsp. butter
2 cups heavy cream or thin béchamel sauce
Salt and pepper

Sprinkle chicken breast with Cajun seasoning and lightly brush with oil and grill until done.

Big Easy Sauce: Sauté diced andouille sausage, crayfish and green onions in butter. Add cream and cook until reduced by 24 percent. Salt and pepper to taste.

Serve chicken on a mound of mashed potatoes with BIG EASY SAUCE.

Chipotle Peppered Steak
Frank Collins

4 Steaks
8 tbsp. Tabasco Chipotle Sauce
2 garlic cloves, crushed
½ tsp. dried oregano
1 ½ tbsp. olive oil
Salt
2 medium red onions, thinly sliced
½ tsp. sugar
½ cup beef broth or heavy cream
Chopped cilantro or parsley for garnish

Coat steaks with mixture of 6 tbsp. of Tabasco, garlic and oregano. Cover and refrigerate for up to 8 hour. Cook steaks add salt and keep them warm, while making sauce. Heat large skillet add oil, add onions and sugar and cook until onions are caramelized, about 5 minutes. Stir in broth or cream, 2 tbsp. Tabasco and ½ tsp. salt. Scrape any bits from side and boil until thickens. Top steaks with onions and garnish.

Meats

Chipotle Rubbed Steaks with Gorgonzola Toast
Stuart Whatley

4 bag leaves
1 ½ tbsp. sweet paprika
1 ½ tsp. Chipotle chili peppers, crushed
¾ tsp. cumin seeds
4 1 inch thick filet-mignon or any boneless cut of meat
1 loaf Ciabatta bread, halved horizontally, cut in half
Olive oil
1 cup creamy gorgonzola cheese
1 tsp. fresh thyme, chopped

Prepare grill, medium high heat. Grind bay leaves, paprika, Chipotle, and cumin seeds, in spice grinder. Reserve 1 teaspoon of mixture. Put remaining mixture on plate. Sprinkle steaks with salt and pepper. Press both sides of steaks into spice mixture in plate, and rub and spread evenly. Grill steaks to preference.

Brush cut sides of bread with olive oil. Grill cut side down until slightly toasted. Spread cheese onto grilled side of each bread slice. Sprinkle top of bread with pepper and reserve spice mixture. Return bread to grill, cheese side up. Grill until cheese melts and bottom is slightly toasted. Remove bread from grill and sprinkle bread with thyme.

Place two slices on 4 plates and serve steak on top.

Cilantro Chili Chicken
Stuart Whatley

2 tbsp. olive oil
2 tbsp. fresh chopped cilantro leaves
1 tbsp. chili powder
1 tbsp. cumin
1 clove garlic (chopped)
2 tsp. salt
½ tsp. black pepper
¼ tsp. cayenne pepper
2 lb. boneless, skinless chicken breast (about 4)
¼ cup green pepper (julienned)
2 tbsp. diced red onions
1 plum tomato, cored and diced
4 oz shredded Monterey Jack pepper cheese

Preheat oven 400°. Mix oil, cilantro, chili powder, cumin, salt, black pepper, garlic, cayenne in bowl, add chicken breast and toss.

Place chicken on foil lined baking sheet, arrange green peppers, onion, and tomato over each piece of chicken.

Cook chicken at 400° for 20 mins. Depending on size of chicken breast make sure that the thickest part of the meat is 165° or more.

Remove chicken and add cheese to melt (make it cheesy). Garnish with fresh cilantro.

Meats

Crown Roast of Pork with Cranberry Dressing

Zoe & Alex Sanders
This recipe came from Zoe's book, <u>Entertaining at the College of Charleston</u>

ROAST:

16 ribs from the rib end of 2 pork loins shaped into crown*
½ tsp. salt
½ tsp. pepper
8 peeled garlic cloves, sliced in half
½ tsp. dried rosemary (or 1 ½ teaspoons fresh)

DRESSING:

1 cup chopped sweet onion
2 tbls. butter
1 lb. bulk milk sausage
1 ½ cups chopped celery
½ cup raisins
½ cup chopped fresh cranberries
2 tart apples, peeled and diced
½ tsp. sage (or 1 ½ teaspoons fresh)
½ tsp. thyme (or 1 ½ teaspoons fresh)
½ tsp. rosemary (or 1 ½ teaspoons fresh)
½ tsp. salt
½ tsp. black pepper
4 cups fresh white bread crumbs
1 cup milk
Parsley or watercress
Cranberries for garnish

TO ROAST:

Sprinkle roast with salt and pepper. Cut slits between every 2 ribs and insert ½ garlic clove. Rub roast with rosemary. Bake at 325° in shallow baking pan until meat begins to pull away from ribs and a meat thermometer inserted into the thickest part of meat, but not touching the bone, register 165° (approximately 20 minutes per pound). Stuff dressing into center of roast 1 hour before removal from oven.

TO MAKE DRESSING:

Sauté onions in butter. Brown sausage and crumble. Drain. Mix onions and sausage with celery, raisins, cranberries, apples, and seasonings. Sauté 5-7 minutes. Moisten bread with milk and squeeze dry. Combine all.

* Have butcher shape roast into a crown. This is a job for a professional. Put little chef caps on each rib after roast is done and garnish with parsley or watercress and fresh cranberries for color.

Cuban Dish

Margaret & Ruddy Attabery

1 whole chicken, cut into serving pieces
1/3 cup oil
1 large onion
1 green pepper
2 cloves garlic
1 cup rice
1 can English peas, drained
1 can tomatoes
8 stuffed olives, chopped
Salt and pepper, to taste
¾ cup beer

Brown chicken pieces in oil. Remove chicken. Sauté the onion, green pepper and garlic. Place chicken in baking dish and cover with rice. Add in sequence peas, tomatoes, and chopped olives. Salt and pepper and beer.

Cook in a 350° preheated oven for 1 hour.

Meats

Enchilada Pie
Frank Beatty

1 ½ lbs. extra lean hamburger meat
1 medium onion, diced
1 can (4oz.) diced green chilies (Ortega works well)
1 can (28 oz.) black olives, drained
2 cans (24 oz. total) pinto beans, drained
8 oz. cheddar cheese, shredded
8 oz. sour cream (non-fat works if desired)
12 corn tortillas
1 bunch scallions, chopped

In a large pot, brown the meat with the onions. Mix in the chilies, enchilada sauce, olives, beans and cheese. Over lap 6 tortillas in the bottom of a large baking pan (10 x 10 is ideal). Spoon roughly half of the saucer-meat-bean mixture over the tortillas. Add the remaining tortillas and top with the remaining mixture. Heat oven to 350° and bake, uncovered, for 20-25 minutes.

Before serving, dollop sour cream and sprinkle scallions all over.

Gamecock Vinegar Pepper Pulled BBQ
Lisa & Eddy Richmond

3/4 cup apple cider vinegar
3/4 cup white vinegar
2 tbls. sugar
¼ cup Worcestershire Sauce
1/2 tsp. red pepper flakes
1 tsp. hot pepper sauce
Salt and pepper

Shred, chop or "pull" pork into shreds with two forks. Add hot pepper vinegar sauce; mix well. Serve on buns with extra sauce and coleslaw, if you choose.

Hamburger Pie
Susie & Heyward King

1 medium onion, chopped
1 lb. ground beef
12 tsp. salt
Dash of pepper
1 No. 2 can green beans
1 (11oz.) can tomato soup
5 medium potatoes, cooked and mashed
½ cup warm milk
1 egg, beaten

Cook onion in small amount of fat. Add meat and seasoning. Brown. Stir in beans and soup. Pour into 1 ½ qt. casserole dish. Combine potatoes, milk, egg and a little salt. Spoon over meat.

Bake at 350° for 30 minutes.

Hungarian Beef Stew
Hannalie & Red Ferguson

1 1/4 lbs. beef stew cubed
1 lb. sliced carrots
2 onions, thinly chopped
3 cups cabbage, thinly sliced
½ cup wine
1 ½ cups water
6 oz. can tomato paste
1 envelope dried onion-mushroom soup mix
1 tbsp. paprika
1 tsp. caraway seeds
1 cup reduced fat sour cream

Combine all ingredients except sour cream in 4 quart slow cooker; mix well. Cover and cook on low for 8 hours. Turn off cooker; stir in sour cream.

Italian Chicken Stew
Pam & Pete Minaya

2 tbls. olive oil
2 stalks celery, cut into bite-size pieces
1 carrot, peeled, cut into bite-size pieces
1 small onion, chopped
Salt and black pepper
1 (14 ½ oz.) can chopped tomatoes
1 (14 oz.) can low-salt chicken broth
½ cup fresh basil leaves, torn into pieces
1 tbsp. tomato paste
1 bay leaf
½ tsp. dried thyme leaves
2 chicken breast with ribs (about 1 ½ pounds total)
1 (15 oz.) can kidney beans (light) drained and rinsed

Heat the olive oil in a heavy 5 ½ quart saucepan over medium heat. Add the celery, carrot, and onion. Sauté the vegetables about 5 minutes. Season with salt and pepper to taste. Stir in the tomatoes with their juices, chicken broth, basil, tomato paste, bay leaf, and thyme. Add the chicken breasts.

Bring to a simmer. Reduce the heat to medium-low and simmer gently uncovered until the chicken is almost cooked through turning the chicken breast over and stirring the mixture occasionally, about 25 minutes. Using tongs transfer the chicken breasts to a work surface and cool for 5 minutes. Discard the bay leaf. Add the kidney beans to the pot and simmer until the liquid has reduced into a stew consistency, about 10 minutes.

Remove the skin and bones from the chicken breasts. Cut the chicken into bite-size pieces. Return the chicken to the stew. Bring the stew just to a simmer. Season with salt and pepper to taste.

Remove the skin and bones from the chicken breasts. Cut the chicken into bite-size pieces. Return the chicken to the stew. Bring the stew just to a simmer. Season with salt and pepper to taste. Serve with salad and bread for an easy and hearty meal.

*If you want a thicker stew add another tablespoon of tomato paste.

Tony Soprano & Mike Dana

Most people don't know that Tony Soprano is a huge Gamecock fan and even fewer people know that Tony has a "boss."

Since the statute of limitation has recently expired we can now divulge the name of that "boss." He is Mike Dana.

Mike and Tony grew up together on Long Island, New York. They were Gumbas. Tony stayed there and Mike decided it best to leave quickly and quietly and headed south.

In Atlanta, Mike Dana (not his real name), posed as a radio salesman for a couple of years while looking for a bar or a joint or whatever, to operate out of.

Meats

It was 27 years ago that he found that "joint." Johnny's Hideaway was the name of it and it still is. "Mikey" doesn't put his "real" name on nothing!

Johnny's Hideaway is on Roswell Road in Atlanta and it is home to a more mature clientele. The median age of its customers is about 60 years old. It is referred to as "God's waiting room."

There is never any trouble in Johnny's Hideaway because a 70 year old "greeter" named Waxy polices the place and nobody fools with Waxy. Places come and places go, but Johnny's Hideaway just stays on forever. Customers die and customers get older to replace them. It's a never-ending cycle. It's an institution.

If you are there on Saturdays in the fall of the year don't ask for Mikey or Tony. They are at the Carolina game, home or away--in disguise.

Italian Sausage with Peppers & Onions
Mike Dana

½ cup fine-quality olive oil
6 sweet Italian sausages
6 hot Italian sausages
6 frying peppers, cored, seeded, and cut, lengthwise, into 1-inch strips
2 large yellow onions, peeled and cut, lengthwise, into ½ inch thick slices
3 garlic coves, peeled and sliced
Salt and pepper to taste

Heat ½ cup oil in large sauté pan over medium-high heat. Add sausages and fry, turning frequently, for about 10 minutes or until sausages are nicely browned.

Stir in peppers, onions, garlic, and salt and pepper. Lower heat and fry for 5 minutes or until vegetables are just tender. Drain off any excess oil and, if desired, remove garlic. Serve with Italian Bread.

Note: We always serve 1 sweet and 1 hot sausage per person. However, you can use any combination of hot and sweet sausages that you prefer. If you don't like heat, use only sweet sausages for a different but just as delicious taste. Any leftovers can be reheated and made into really great sandwiches served on crusty Italian bread.

Kathi's "Killer" Meatloaf
Kathi & Jimmy Mitchell

¼ cup milk
1 medium onion, chopped finely
½ cup ketchup
1 tsp. salt
1 cup Italian flavored breadcrumbs
2 ½ lbs. ground beef
½ cup bell pepper
1 egg, beaten
½ tsp. black pepper

Sauce:
½ cup tomato sauce, (Italian style with basil)
3 tbsp. brown sugar
2 tbsp. prepared mustard

Preheat oven to 350°. Mix all ingredients together. Shape into a loaf and place in baking pan. Mix together the sauce ingredients and pour over the meatloaf. Bake for 1 hour or until done.

Jennifer, Kristy, Cocky, Trish and Becky

Marinated Flank Steak
Trish & Warren Norris

¾ cup vegetable oil
¼ cup soy sauce
½ cup honey
2 tbls. vinegar
2 tbls. chopped onion
1/8 tsp. garlic salt
¼ tsp. ginger
1 ½ to 2 lbs. flank steak

Combine all ingredients except flank steak. Place flank steak in a plastic ziploc bag and pour marinade over top. Close bag and chill at least four hours. Broil meat five minutes on each side or to taste. Cut in diagonal strips and serve. Great for tailgating, leave the meat in the cooler in the ziploc bag until ready to grill.

Marinated Pork Roast
Mary Ella Wright

1 4-6 lb. pork loin boned, rolled and tied
2 tbls. dry mustard
2 tsp. thyme
2 cloves garlic minced
1 tsp. ginger
½ cup dry sherry
½ cup soy sauce

Place meat in large plastic bag. Combine mustard, thyme, garlic, ginger, sherry and soy sauce. Blend well. Pour marinade over roast. Marinade in refrigerator 1-2 days. Turning occasionally.

Place meat in shallow pan. Bake uncovered at 350° allowing 30 minutes per pound. Baste often with marinade. Serve with apricot sauce.

Apricot Sauce:
  Yield 1 ½ cups.
  1 10 oz. jar apricot preserves
  1 tbsp. soy sauce
  2 tbsp. dry sherry

Heat slowly in small saucepan until preserves are melted.

Mary Lou's Pot Roast
Pam & Pete Minaya

1 (2-3 lb.) boneless beef chuck roast
1 tsp. salt
½ tsp. pepper
3 tbsp. all-purpose flour
3 tbsp. vegetable oil

Sprinkle roast with salt, pepper, and 3 tablespoons flour. Brown all sides of roast in hot oil in a large Dutch oven. Reduce heat to low and remove roast and set aside.

Add:
- I cup of beef broth
- I pkg. of Lipton's Onion Soup Mix to

Dutch oven drippings; stirring well. Return roast to Dutch oven and layer the top of roast with sliced onion. Cover and simmer over low heat for 2 hours.

Cut 4 potatoes and 3 carrots in bit size pieces and place around roast. Cover and cooked until vegetables are tender.

Mom's Chicken
Beverly & Herman Hill

- 2- 3 lb. chicken fryers
- I cup water- or more
- I cup sherry or vermouth
- ½ tsp. curry
- ½ cup celery
- I onion, sliced
- 2 6 oz. Uncle Ben's Wild Rice
- I lb. fresh mushrooms
- I stick butter
- I cup sour cream
- I can cream of mushroom soup

Combine and simmer 1st six ingredients I hour. Remove chicken and save liquid. Cook rice with liquid while deboning chicken. Slice and sauté mushrooms in I stick of butter. Mix together chicken rice, mushrooms with sour cream and soup. Pour in casserole dish; cook 30 minutes in 350°oven.

College of Charleston's "Mystery Meat"
Zoe & Alex Sanders
This recipe came from Zoe's book,
Entertaining at the College of Charleston

This recipe will turn a truly disgusting piece of meat - one that looks like a random animal which has been hit by a truck, i.e., a "road kill"-into something really grand. The pineapple juice will tenderize a MICHELIN radial. The recipe is entirely suitable for all kinds of meat. (This is Alex's recipe.)

- 5-6 lb. slab of meat from an indefinite origin (venison, elk, moose, buffalo, or if you insist, beef chuck roast)
- 3 large (46-oz.) cans pineapple juice
- 3 lbs. beef suet or pork fat (substitute, if you must, I lb. bacon)
- 4 tbsp. salt
- 4 tbsp. black pepper
- 12 large Wadmalaw Sweet Onions cut into half-rings (may substitute Vidalias)
- 4 tbsp. plus I tsp. hot dog mustard (no substitute)
- I tbsp. Kitchen Bouquet
- 3 cups all-purpose flour
- ½ cup red wine
- 12 cups beef bouillon
- 4 dashes Worcestershire sauce
- I bay leaf
- Chopped parsley

Wrap meat in clean bath towel, put in large pan, pour pineapple juice over, refrigerate and marinate 6 hours. Melt fat in iron skillet or frying pan. Remove cracklings.

Sprinkle I tablespoon salt and I tablespoon pepper over onions. Sauté onions in fat until soft. Remove onions. Add 4 tablespoons salt and 3 tablespoons pepper on meat. Cover with flour on both sides and pound vigorously with rolling pin. Brown meat on both sides in remaining fat (you may have to add vegetable oil.) Transfer meat to Dutch oven.

Deglaze frying pan with wine. Pour in 6 cups bouillon, Worcestershire sauce, and bay leaf. Make sure bouillon mixture is under the meat as well as around it. Simmer on the lowest possible heat that will keep pan barely bubbling until tender (approximately 3-4 hours).

Add bouillon as necessary to keep sufficient liquid in pan. Bouillon mixture will automatically become the gravy. Put one teaspoon of mustard and chopped parsley on top for color.

Nide's Duck Tetrazzini
Dottie & Buddy Nidiffer

1 Whole Duck
1 lb. Spaghetti paste
Flour-All purpose
Butter
Broth

Salt and Pepper
White Onion, large
Celery
Cheese

Boil duck breast in water, onion, celery, salt and pepper until meat is tender. Cool. Pull meat from bones. Save broth.

WHITE SAUCE:
1 stick of butter
¼ cup flour
2 ½ cups broth

Melt butter and add flour. Stir thoroughly. Add broth and continue to stir. When thick and smooth add meat. Cook and drain spaghetti paste. Combine all of the above and place in rectangular baking dish and top with grated Parmesan cheese or the cheese of your choice.

Bake at 400° for 15-20 minutes or until cheese has melted.

Note: You can substitute the flour and about half of the broth for any cream of chicken, mushroom, or celery soups. You can also substitute the meat for dove, quail or chicken. It is very good, as well as a little moister, with white and dark meat combination.
Serves: 6-8. Male friends and family especially love this dish.

Northshore Jambalaya
Frank Beatty

½ lb. pork tenderloin, chopped
½ lb. smoked sausage, ½ inch slices
¼ cup vegetable oil

¼ cup all-purpose flour
1 cup celery, chopped
1 cup onion, chopped
1 cup green onions, chopped
4 garlic cloves, minced
1 tbsp. parsley, chopped
1 can (8 oz.) tomato paste
1 tsp. garlic salt
½ tsp. black pepper
½ tsp. Hungarian paprika
½ tsp. dried thyme
½ tsp. red pepper
6 cups uncooked rice

Cook sausage and pork until browned; drain well and set aside. Cook rice according to package directions and set aside. Heat oil in large stock or soup pot; add flour and cook over medium-high heat, stirring constantly, until roux turns dark brown. Stir in onion, celery, half of green onions, garlic and parsley. Cook 10 minutes over medium heat, stirring frequently. Add tomato sauce and seasonings. Reduce heat and simmer 5 minutes, stirring occasionally. Stir in sausage and pork and remaining green onions. Cook until thoroughly heated. Add cooked rice and mix well. Simmer covered for 5 minutes or until contents are heated through.

Recipe can be made a couple of days ahead and heated on game day.

Pork Tenderloins with Orange Sauce
Connie & Stan Smith

2 pork tenderloins, 2 lbs. each
2 tbsp. butter
¾ cup chopped onion
2 tsp. salt
¼ tsp. pepper
½ cup white wine
3 oranges, squeezed, a fourth orange to be used later
1 bay leaf
1 tbsp. chopped parsley
1 ½ tsp. cornstarch
4 cups, hot cooked rice

Sauté tenderloins in butter until golden brown. Remove from pan and cook onion, salt and pepper in butter until tender. Return meat to pan and pour wine and juice of oranges over meat and add sugar, bay leaf crumbled and parsley. Cover pan and simmer until meat is tender (about 45 minutes). Peel and section the 4th orange, cut and peel in very thin strips and boil in small amount of water until tender. Mix cornstarch with a small amount of water (1 tablespoon) and add to broth, stirring constantly until thick and smooth. Cut tenderloin in thick slices and arrange in platter with rice. Pour sauce over meat, garnish with orange peel.

Roasted Chicken with Balsamic Vinaigrette
Stuart Whatley

¼ cup balsamic vinegar
2 tbls. Dijon mustard
2 tbls. fresh lemon juice
2 garlic cloves, chopped
2 tbls. olive oil
Salt and freshly ground black pepper
1 (4 pound) whole chicken, cut into pieces (giblets, neck and backbone reserved for another use)
½ cup low-salt chicken broth
1 tsp. lemon zest
1 tbsp. chopped fresh parley leaves

Whisk the vinegar, mustard, lemon juice, garlic, olive oil, salt and pepper in small bowl to blend. Combine the vinaigrette and chicken pieces in a large resealable plastic bag and toss to coat. Refrigerate turning the chicken pieces occasionally, for at least 2 hours and up to 1 day.

Preheat the oven to 400°. Remove chicken from the bag and arrange the chicken pieces on a large greased baking dish. Roast until the chicken is just cooked through, about 1 hour. If your chicken browns too quickly, cover it with foil for the remaining cooking time. Transfer the chicken to a serving platter. Place the baking dish on a burner over medium-low heat. Whisk the chicken broth into the pan drippings, scraping up any browned bits on the bottom of the baking sheet with a wooden spoon and mixing them into the broth and pan drippings. Drizzle the pan drippings over the chicken. Sprinkle the lemon zest and parsley over the chicken, and serve.

Rosemary Lamb Chops
Kathi & Jimmy Mitchell

½ cup olive oil
½ cup teriyaki sauce
½ cup balsamic vinegar
8 garlic cloves, minced
4 tsp dried rosemary
8- ¾ inch thick lamb chops

Whisk together first five ingredients. Place lamb chops in a 9x13x2 inch pan. Pour marinade over top. Let stand at room temperature 30 to 45 minutes or chill 2 to 3 hours. Remove chops from marinade, discarding marinade.

Grill oven medium heat 3 to 4 minutes on each side for medium rare.
Serves 4

Elizabeth & Bill Jerry

Bill was a three year letterman (1957-58-59) at USC. Bill and his wife, Elizabeth, are the owners of the Mouse Trap Restaurant and Bar, located just off Forest Drive. They have been there for 27 years. The Mouse Trap is a hang out for a more mature clientele. Bill told me recently that he could attend two funerals a week for his regular customers. This means he will be out of business in just 20 years.

Savory Baked Pork Chops
Elizabeth & Bill Jerry

    4 large pork chops
    Salt & pepper
    Small amount of oil

SAUCE:
    ¼ cup vegetable or olive oil
    1 large onion
    1 red and one green bell pepper, coarsely chopped
    ¼ cup flour
    1 can beef broth
    1 can chicken broth
    ½ tsp. each, sage, rosemary and thyme

Salt and pepper the pork chops and brown on a flat grill or frying pan with small amount of oil.

For the sauce:
Sauté onion until clear. Add red and green peppers. Remove from heat. Add flour and stir. To this add the cans of broth and herbs. Bring to a slow boil just until slightly thickened. Pour over chops and bake at 300° to 325° for about an hour. Sauce should reduce and thicken slightly.

Stu's Butt Roast
Stuart Whatley

    10-12 lb. Pork Roast, bone out
    Apple juice
    Butt Rub

Butt Rub:
    2 cups salt
    2 cups sugar
    2 cups brown sugar
    2 cups ground cumin
    2 cups chili powder
    2 cups black pepper
    1 cup cayenne pepper
    4 cups paprika
    Mix well. You will have a lot left over for later use.

Rub down pork roast with Butt Rub real good. Let sit in refrigerator overnight.

Prepare grill for indirect heat cooking at 225° (put hot coals to one side of grill or only use one side for gas grills).

Take roast and place on cool side of grill. Close lid and monitor temperature of grill so that it stays at

225°. Try not to peek. Cook roast on grill for 10 hours spraying roast with apple juice every 2 hours (will need clean spray bottle). After 10 hours wrap roast in tin foil, and let sit in grill for an hour. Then take roast, in foil, out and wrap in clean towel and place in a cooler (no ice, just empty cooler). Let sit in cooler for another hour. Trust me, all of this will make for the tenderest roast you've ever put in your mouth. Pull meat from roast and add to favorite BBQ sauce or eat dry. So good it'll make your head sag in.

USC Chicken Spread
Lisa & Eddy Richmond

1 can cooked chicken, shredded or chopped small
1 16 oz. pkg. cream cheese (softened)
4 tbsp. Worcestershire sauce
Pinch of salt/pepper to taste
Add any herb you like.

Mix all together.

Meats

Seafood

Achiote Grilled Shrimp - Frank Beatty

Bailey Tailgating Menu - Carolina & Don Bailey

Baked Patstry Covered Salmon - Jerri & Steve Spurrier

Cheesy Shrimp & Grits - Linda Flowers

Crab or Shrimp Stuffing for Fish - Frank Collins

Breakfast Shrimp - Hootie Johnson

Fabulous Feta Shrimp - Kathy & Jimmy Mitchell

Free Style Flounder - Frank Collins

Grilled Fish with Garlic Mayonnaise - Roy Beasley

Grouper with Lemon Beurre Blanc - Litchfield Plantation

Herb Coated Baked Fish - Tom & Margaret Price

Imperial Crab - Ruth Grantz

Low Country Shrimp Gravy - Elaine & Weemie Baskins

Oyster Holy Moses - Frank Collins

Scallops Pianissimo - Frank Collins

Short Cut Seafood Soup - Jane & Tommy Suggs

Shrimp & Wild Rice Casserole - Orral Anne & Jim Moss

Spot Tail Bass - Roy & Ginger McLaurin

Achiote Grilled Shrimp
Frank Beatty

¾ cup freshly squeezed orange juice (about 2 naval or anges)
2 tbsp. achiote paste (see note below)
1 tbsp. freshly squeezed lime juice
2 garlic cloves, minced
½ tsp. cumin
Freshly cracked black pepper
24 shrimp, peeled and deveined

Prepare grill and 8 (8 inch) skewers for grilling.

In the bowl of a blender, combine orange juice, achiote paste, lime juice, garlic, cumin and black pepper; process about 1 minute or until free of lumps. Fold in shrimp; cover and chill for about 30 minutes.

Drain shrimp and discard marinade. Thread 3 shrimp onto each of the 8 skewers. Grill shrimp about 2 minutes per side until just done.

Note: Achiote paste is typically available in small packages at Latin American markets. The color of achiote paste is very concentrated. In order to avoid staining your fingertips, wear a pair of clean, disposable gloves when threading the shrimp onto the skewers.
This recipe makes about 4 servings.

Donald Bailey

A three year letterman for the Gamecocks (1968-69-70). Donald has the dubious honor of having the second longest interception return that did not result in a touchdown. It was 90 yards for nothing

Bailey Tailgating Menu
Caroline & Don Bailey

Beer Boiled Lowcountry Shrimp
Peel and Clean
Dip in mixture of ketchup and mayonnaise with spices of your choice
Serve with raw oysters over saltine crackers
Drink cold beer and wine

Baked Pastry Covered Salmon
Jerri & Steve Spurrier

Large Salmon
Pepperidge Farm Puff Pastry
Shrimp, crab, scallops, precooked
Salt & Pepper to taste
Shrimp Soup
Sherry

Season Salmon and wrap with Puff Pastry. Bake till brown at 350° for about 20 minutes.

Cover with mixture of seafood, soup and some sherry.

Serve with sliced tomatoes and parsley.

Cook shrimp in same pan over medium high heat 3 minutes or until almost pink, stirring occasionally. Add lemon juice and next 4 ingredients, and cook 3 minutes. Stir in bacon.

Spoon grits onto individual plates or into shallow bowls; top with shrimp mixture.
Serve immediately.
Serves 4

Cheesy Shrimp and Grits
Billy Canada & Linda Flowers

3 cups chicken broth
1 cup uncooked quick-cooking grits
½ tsp. salt
¼ tsp. freshly ground pepper
2 tbsp. butter
2 cups (8 oz.) shredded Cheddar cheese
6 slices bacon, chopped
2 lbs. medium shrimp, peeled and deveined
1 tbsp. fresh lemon juice
2 tsp. Worcestershire sauce
2 tbsp. chopped fresh parsley
6 green onions, chopped
2 garlic cloves, minced

Bring chicken broth to a boil over medium high heat; stir in grits. Cook, stirring occasionally, 5 to 7 minutes or until thickened. Remove from heat; stir in salt and next 3 ingredients. Set aside, and keep warm.

Cook bacon in a large nonstick skillet over medium high heat 3 minutes or until crisp; remove bacon from pan.

Crab or Shrimp Stuffing for Fish
Frank Collins

½ lb. boiled shrimp or
¼ lb. crabmeat
¼ loaf bread, crumbled including crusts
¼ bunch parsley, minced
1 egg
¼ cup butter
½ bunch green onions, tops only
¼ cup sherry
Salt and pepper
2 garlic cloves, minced

Stuffing: Mix together bread crumbs, minced shrimp, crabmeat, and minced parsley. Melt butter in saucepan, sauté green onion tops until softened but not thoroughly cooked, add sherry and heat for a few seconds. Beat egg and add with salt and pepper.

Hootie Johnson

The ex-Chairman of Augusta National was a three-year South Carolina football letterman. Hootie played in the shadows of Bishop Strickland and Steve Wadiak, two of the greatest running backs in Gamecock history. But as a blocker he excelled. He won the Jacobs Blocking Trophy in his senior year. At 35, Johnson became the youngest bank president ever in S.C.

Breakfast Shrimp
Hootie Johnson

Special flavor is given this Carolina favorite by sautéing the shrimp in bacon fat instead of butter.

¼ cup onion, chopped
2 tbs. green bell pepper, chopped
2 tbls. bacon drippings
2 lbs. medium-size shrimp, shelled
1 ½ cups water
3 tbs. all-purpose flour, combined with 1 to 2 tbs. water
Salt and freshly ground pepper, to taste
2 tsp. worcestershire sauce
3 tbs. chili sauce

Sauté onion and bell pepper in drippings until golden. Add shrimp and cook, stirring, 1 to 2 minutes, until opaque.

Add water; simmer 2 to 3 minutes. Thicken with flour and water mixture. Add salt, pepper, worcestershire sauce, and chili sauce. Simmer 2 to 3 minutes until thick.

Jimmy Mitchell

Jimmy was one of USC's all-time best receivers. He was an All-ACC selection in 1970 and was the Gamecocks' leading receiver in 1970 and 1971 with 88 catches for 1,460 yards. Jimmy is now a custom home builder which means he builds houses for rich people.

Fabulous Feta Shrimp
Kathi & Jimmy Mitchell

2 lbs. fresh shrimp, peeled and deveined
3 garlic cloves, finely chopped
1 tbsp. olive oil
2 tbsp. white wine
1 16 oz. can diced tomatoes, drained

Dash of salt and pepper
½ cup crumbled feta cheese
Hot cooked rice

Sauté shrimp and garlic in hot oil in a skillet; add wine and cook until shrimp is opaque. Add tomatoes, salt and pepper. Cook for 1 minute. Transfer to a serving dish and top with feta cheese.

Serve over hot cooked rice.

Free Style Flounder
Frank Collins

4 Flounder

Marinade:
½ cup dry white wine
1 tbsp. olive oil
Juice of 1 lemon
Dash of soy sauce

Tomato Mixture:
6 cherry tomatoes, quartered
1 clove garlic, 1 shallot, both minced
1 small red onion, minced
1 dozen capers

Marinate tomato mixture for one hour. Take all ingredients and heat in sauce pan on medium heat for 5 minutes. Preheat oven to 500 degrees. Place 2 flounder filets in a baking dish and lightly season with salt. After the tomato mixture has cooled, pour over the flounder and bake until just done, about 10 minutes. Serve with herbed rice. Herbed rice add 1 tsp. each fresh basil, thyme and oregano. Add 2 tbsp. olive oil to brown rice with 2 cups chicken stock or water. Also add 2 tsp. sea salt or kosher salt.

Alex, Rose, Roy Beasley & Charlie

Senator Beasley, as he refers to himself, has got to be the smartest man in Barnwell County. How else can you explain it? He has been hustling the same golfing buddies for 50 years.

When I first moved to Denmark, I called Heyward King in Lake City and told him I had moved to Denmark. The first words out of Heyward's mouth were "don't ever play golf with Roy Beasley for money." That is how infamous Roy Beasley is in the state of South Carolina.

About a year ago Roy broke his leg and could not play golf for five or six months. During this time his golf game had deteriorated. Over drinks he told me that he was depressed, "Alex," he said, "my golf game is gone, my career might be over."

Well he's back! As of this writing, Roy has recovered, modified his game and is once again dangerous on the links.

He lives by his own moral code and what he

Seafood

Cookin' with Cocky II

doesn't break, he bends. So look out for Senator Beasley and if you have to gamble with him, I suggest you play gin rummy.

Grilled Fish with Garlic Mayonnaise
Roy Beasley

4 fish steaks, 1–inch thick, 6 to 8 oz. each (halibut, salmon, etc.)
3 cloves garlic
1 ½ tsp. paprika
½ tsp. ground red pepper
1 tsp. salt
½ cup mayonnaise

Place garlic, paprika red pepper, and salt in blender. Add ¼ cup mayonnaise, process until garlic is minced and mixed into sauce. Add remaining mayonnaise and process until smooth. Spread 1 to 2 tsp. sauce on each side of fish steak.

Grill in very hot skillet, or broil 4 to 5 minutes until lightly brown. Turn. Brown other side 4 to 5 minutes. For well done fish, lower heat. Grill or broil 4 to 5 minutes longer.
Arrange fish on platter or serving plates.

Garnish with cooked asparagus or whole green beans, lemon halves, and dill springs.

Grouper with Lemon Beurre Blanc
Courtesy of Litchfield Plantation

1 garlic clove, minced
1 ½ shallots, sliced
2 cups white wine
1 fresh thyme sprig
1 bay leaf
1 ½ tsp. whole white peppercorns
2 cups heavy cream
1 oz. cornstarch slurry
1 ½ lbs. whole butter, diced large
3 tbsp. fresh lemon juice
4 8-oz. grouper filets
Salt and pepper
Flour
1 oz. clarified butter

In heavy saucepan combine garlic, shallots, white wine, thyme, bay leaf, and peppercorns. Bring to simmer and reduce until dry. Add heavy cream; reduce by half. Add the cornstarch slurry and bring to simmer, simmer 5 minutes. Reduce heat and slowly whip in whole butter until emulsified. Finish the sauce with the lemon juice; salt to taste. Season grouper filet with salt and pepper. Coat fillets lightly with flour. Pan-sear in clarified butter, about 5 minutes on each side. Add sauce to pan and continue cooking 2 more minutes. Serve immediately.

Seafood

Tom & Margaret Price

Tom enrolled at Carolina in January 1948 at age 21 after a four-year hitch in the U. S. Navy. Another Navy veteran enrolled the same day: His name was Steve Wadiak.

He graduated in June 1951 with bachelor of arts degree in journalism and worked nearly 11 years for United Press International as the South Carolina bureau manager. He returned to Carolina in April 1962 as sports information director and retired after nearly 31 years at end of 1992 and has since hung around as part-time consultant and Gamecock historian.

Tom authored five books on Gamecock athletic: Fire Ants & Black Magic (1985), A Century of Gamecocks/Memorable Football Moments (1995), A Century of Gamecock/Memorable Basketball Moments (1996), A Century of Gamecocks/ Memorable Baseball Moments (1996), and Tales From the Gamecock Roost (2001).

He married Margaret Fletcher of Charleston in June 1950 and they have been happily married since.

They have three children, two of them Carolina graduated (one with four degrees) and are presently college professors (Ball State/Indiana, University of Staffordshire/England). The other one is the ultimate Gamecock fan who tailgates and serves Gator meat when Carolina plays Florida. Tom has three grandchildren and one great-grandchild.

He first saw a Carolina football game versus the Charleston Coast Guard in 1943 just before joining the Navy, and saw his first Carolina-Clemson game in 1947 (21-19 Cocks win). He has witnessed 59 consecutive Gamecock-Tiger games through 2005.

Tom has been invaluable to us in writing our cookbooks. He is the foremost authority on Carolina football and has saved me countless hours of research. He is a true Hall of Famer.

Herb Coated Baked Fish
Tom & Margaret Price

6 (4 to 6 ounces each) fish filets
4 scallions (green onions)
½ cup freshly grated Parmesan cheese
½ cup mayonnaise (Hellman's preferred)
½ cup of dry breadcrumbs
1 tsp. dried basil
1 tsp. dried oregano
¼ tsp. salt
¼ tsp. black pepper

Select six fish filets. Good with any white flesh fish such as grouper, flounder, tilapia, etc. Also good with salmon. Line a baking sheet with foil and spray lightly with Pam. Preheat oven to 400°.

Finely chop about four scallions or green onions. Combine with grated Parmesan cheese and mayonnaise. Spread mixture evenly over fish on the foil lined baking sheet.

In a separate bowl, combine dry breadcrumbs, dried basil, dried oregano, salt and pepper. Sprinkle this mixture over the coated fish filets.

Place in oven and bake for 10 minutes. Serve with green salad, side dish and crusty bread. Enjoy

Imperial Crab
Ruth Grantz

1 lb. Back Fin Lump Crab Meat
3 tbsp. mayonnaise
1 egg
1 tbsp. lemon juice
½ tbsp. Worcestershire Sauce
½ tbsp. parsley flakes
1 ½ tbsp. melted butter
1 tsp. Old Bay Seafood Seasoning

Mix ingredients. Fill crab shells. Top with small amount of cracker crumbs covered with melted butter. Sprinkle with paprika.

Bake at 350° for 15 – 20 minutes.

Weemie & Elaine Baskins, Doug Hatcher, Buddy Mayfield & Dwight Keith

Weemie Baskins

How does Weemie do it? That is a question I have been asking for 50 years. How did he remain a starting receiver at USC for three years without ever catching a pass? How did he get and keep the job of Special Investigator of Trade Research for the Coca-Cola Company for five years? How did Weemie get into my hotel room at 3 a.m. in San Francisco in 1960? How did Weemie become an "Art Dealer" and make a living at it for 10 years?

How did Weemie know that the Vista was going to be a hot spot 20 years before anyone else? When he opened Bryan's Warehouse there in 1976, it was the only restaurant in the Vista. How did Weemie get elected to the South Carolina General Assembly in 1972?

Just a little over 10 years ago, Weemie got tired of the "pioneering" business and married his wife, Elaine. They are in the more subdued business of Pet Sitting.

Seafood

Low Country Shrimp Gravy
Elaine & Weemie Baskins

1 lb. sausage
1 lg. onion
2-3 stalks celery and leaves
1 bunch parsley
½ cup flour or gravy mix
1 bay leaf
2 tbsp. Creole or Old Bay Seasoning
4-5 tbsp. Worcestershire
Salt, pepper, chili powder to taste
2-3 lbs. medium shrimp

Stir everything together, mixing and tossing well, adjust seasoning…Cover and let it bubble…cook grits or rice…raise temp from low to medium.. stir in shrimp…cook 5 min…serve over grits or rice…freezes well. (without shrimp).

Oysters Holy Moses
Frank Collins

1 dozen shucked oysters
3 cups peanut oil

BREADING:
1 cup high gluten flour
½ cup fine cracker meal
1 tbsp. each: salt, black pepper, paprika
2 tsp. cayenne pepper

FIRECRACKER SAUCE:
1 tbsp. olive oil
12 cup finely minced yellow onion
½ cup chopped red onion
2 jalapeno peppers, chopped with ½ seeds
1 red sweet pepper, chopped
1 tsp. fresh chopped parsley
2 cups fresh tomato puree

1 tsp. each salt, sugar, cayenne, pepper, oregano

Sauté all ingredients for the sauce except the puree and seasoning over medium heat until all are tender, add puree and seasonings, simmer on low for 20 minutes. Dust oysters with breading and fry for 1 ½ minutes.

Scallops Pianissimo
Frank Collins

1 lb. sea scallops
1 cup each: julienne celery, tender leeks green & white or shallots
½ stick butter
½ cup white wine
½ cup water or clam broth
1 lemon
3 tbsp. fresh tarragon or 1 ½ dried
½ to ¾ cup heavy cream
3 tbsp. all purpose flour

Put julienne vegetables in a large saucepan or skillet. Add butter, wine and water or clam broth; then tarragon, salt and pepper. Put circle of wax paper over vegetables to help them "sweat". For 10-15 min. Quickly sauté scallops over high heat in 3 tbsp. butter. Remove from pan and keep warm, sprinkle with salt and pepper. Add remaining butter to scallop pan. When butter bubbles add flour to make a roux. Stir for 3 to 5 minutes until flour is cooked but not browned. Add some cooking liquid from the vegetables, a little wine and finish with cream until a tin sauce is made. Season with salt and more fresh tarragon.

To Serve: Divide vegetables among plates, put scallops over vegetables with white sauce. Garnish with fresh tarragon.

FIRECRACKER SAUCE:
1 tbsp. olive oil
12 cup finely minced yellow onion
½ cup chopped red onion
2 jalapeno peppers, chopped with ½ seeds
1 red sweet pepper, chopped
1 tsp. fresh chopped parsley
2 cups fresh tomato puree
1 tsp. each salt, sugar, cayenne, pepper, oregano

Sauté all ingredients for the sauce except the puree and seasoning over medium heat until all are tender, add puree and seasonings, simmer on low for 20 minutes. Dust oysters with breading and fry for 1 ½ minutes.

Tommy Suggs

Tommy shares the record for the most touchdown passes in one game. He threw for 4,916 yards and 34 touchdowns...all of those marks were once records and now rank second behind Todd Ellis. More importantly, he never lost to Clemson. Tommy is in his 34th year as a color analyst for the Gamecock football network.

Short Cut Seafood Soup
Jane & Tommy Suggs

1 dozen shucked oysters
3 cups peanut oil

BREADING:
1 cup high gluten flour
½ cup fine cracker meal
1 tbsp. each: salt, black pepper, paprika
2 tsp. cayenne pepper

Orral Anne & Jim Moss

Wild and reckless on and off the field, Jim has mellowed some. He plays some golf and is a practicing attorney in Beaufort.

Shrimp & Wild Rice Casserole
Orral Anne & Jim Moss

1 box Uncle Ben's long grain and wild rice
1 can cream of celery soup
1 tbsp. green pepper, chopped
1 small onion, chopped
2 tbsp. butter, melted
1 tbsp. lemon juice
½ tbsp. Worcestershire sauce
½ tsp. dry mustard
¼ tsp. pepper
½ cup mild cheese, cubed
½ lb. uncooked shrimp

Cook rice by package directions. Peel and clean shrimp. If using a deep dish cook shrimp a tiny bit. Add all other ingredients to rice, drain shrimp and add to mixture. Put in greased casserole dish.
Bake 375° for 35 minutes, uncovered.

This recipe can be put together a day ahead in a large zip lock bag, refrigerate. Take out and put in baking dish and cook when needed. Can also be taken to a function and kept hot by wrapping in heavy tin foil, then wrapping in a heavy towel. It will stay warm for several hours.

Shrimp In Mustard Sauce
Shari McKissick

2 ½ lbs. shrimp, shelled and deveined
¼ cup parsley, finely chopped
¼ cup green onions, finely chopped
1 cup tarragon vinegar
½ cup olive oil
4 tsp. Dijon-style mustard
2 tsp. crushed red pepper
1 tsp. salt
Fresh ground pepper

Cook shrimp in boiling water to cover just until they turn pink. Drain and transfer to a large bowl. Mix the remaining ingredients together and pour over warm shrimp. Mix well so every shrimp will be coated. Cover and refrigerate. Serve in a bowl with toothpicks.

Spot Tail Bass
Roy & Ginger McLaurin

This is one of our favorites (because Roy loves to catch spot tail bass!)-this is particularly good for fancy guest.

Spot tail bass filets
1 ½ cups of sour cream
¾ cup mayonnaise
¾ cup finely chopped onion
Paprika to taste

Spray a shallow baking dish with Pam Non-Stick Spray. Place filets in the baking dish and sprinkle with a little lemon juice and salt and pepper. Cover with a mixture of sour cream, mayonnaise and chopped onions. Sprinkle top with paprika and bake 350° for 15 to 20 minutes.

Desserts

Four Layer Choclate Delight - Ria & Edwin Floyd
Almond Pound Cake - Frances Sloan Fulmer
Banana Fritters - Frank Beatty
Banana Pudding - Van & Susan Mullis
Banana Split Dessert - Renee & Ed Holler
Better Than Sex Cake - Frances Sloan Fulmer
Blueberry Pound Cake - Sandra & Howard Hughes
Brittle - Lisa Dievendorf
Butter Pecan Crunch - Margaret & Tom Price
Candy Bar Pie - Frances Sloan Fulmer
Caramel Brownies - Ben & Louise Galloway
Charlotte Russe - Lynn Steedman
Cheesecake - Jan & Billy Gambrell
Chocoalte Bread Pudding - Linda Flowers
Chocolate Caramel Pecan Cheesecake - Lucy Hughes
Chocolate Chip Cheesecake Ball - Kaye Hunke
Chocolate E'clair Cake - Ruth Grantz
Chocolate Pound Cake - Mary Hughes
Coconut Cake - Pauline & Eric Hyman
Coconut Squares - Vann & Susan Mullis
Colin's Pinto Beans Geechie Pie - Colin Ayers
Cream Cheese Lemon Squares - Sandra & Howard Hughes
Cream Cheese-Topped Pineapple Cake - J.R. Wilburn
Cream Pound Cake - Orral Anne & Jim Moss
Debbie's Banana & Oreo Surprise - Debbie Faulk
Dreama's Fruit Cake - Dreama Sue Osborne
Dreama's Old Timey Sweets - Dreama Suse Osborne

Dump Cake - Frances Sloan Fulmer
Easy Banana Pudding - Betsy Collins
Easy Egg Custard Pie - Al Johnson
English Toffee - Margaret & Tom Price
Gamecock Brittle - Debbie Faulk
Gloria's Blueberry Pie - M.R. & Sonny Edwards
Heath Bar Cake - Andrea Bailey
Huquenot Torte - Margaret & Ruddy Attaberry
Lemon Cookies - Frances Sloan Fulmer
Lemon Jell-O Pound Cake - Emily White
Little Cheesecakes - Pam Harrison
Lusious Lemon Pie - Kathi & Jimmy Mitchell
Marion's Apple Pie - Van & Susan Mullis
Melt in Your Mouth Pecan Pie - Tom & Margaret Price
Million Dollar Pound Cake - Debbie & Durry Faulk
Mitchell's Mocha Cheesecake - Kathi & Jimmy Mitchell
My Mother's Pound Cake - Cathy Hughes
Pecan Pralines - Margaret & Tom Price
Plantation Pecan Crunch - Magaret & Tom Price
Pralines - Margaret & Tom Price
Punch Bowl Cake - Ria & Edwin Floyd
Quick & Easy Cheesecake - Susan Hughes
Rice Crispy Peanut Butter - M&M Treats - Mary Kay & Chip Wilson
Ruby Slipper Cake - Cheryl Wheat
Skillet Pineapple Upside-Down Cake - Pam & Pete Minaya
Strawberry Cake - LTC Alfred Johnson
Sweet Tea Pie - Frank Beatty

Four Layer Chocolate Delight
Ria & Edwin Floyd

First Layer:
    2 sticks of butter
    2 cups Self-rising flour
    I cup pecans, chopped

Pat in bottom of pan and bake at 350° for 20 minutes.

Second Layer:
    I large cream cheese. I use one 8 oz and one 3 oz package.
    I cup powdered sugar
    2 cups Cool Whip

Third Layer:
    2 packages chocolate Instant Pudding
    3 cups milk

Fourth Layer:
    Spread 2 cups of Cool Whip on top
    Grate one large Hershey Bar and add to the top.

Almond Pound Cake
Frances Sloan Fulmer

    I stick soft margarine
    3 cups cake flour
    5 eggs
    I cup milk
    I cup shortening
    3 cups sugar
    ½ tsp. baking powder
    I tbsp. each of vanilla and almond extracts

Cream shortening and sugar with a mixer. Add eggs one at a time, mixing after each addition. In a sep-arate container, add vanilla and almond flavorings to milk. In another container, add baking powder to sifted flour. Alternately add 1/3 of the flour mixture and ½ of the milk mixture to the creamed shortening and sugar. Pour the batter into a well greased, floured tube pan. Place in a cold oven. Turn oven to 325°, and bake for I hour and 25 minutes. Let cool 10 to 15 minutes.

Banana Fritters
Frank Beatty

Batter:
    2 cups all-purpose flour
    I tbl. baking powder
    I egg
    I tbsp. cooking oil
    ¾ cup sweet condensed milk
    ½ cup water
    I pinch salt

Combine all ingredients and mix well. Set aside until ready for use.

Bananas:
    5 bananas, peeled and cut diagonally
    2 tbsp. sugar
    Juice of one fresh lime
    3 tbsp. dark rum
    Caramel or chocolate dipping sauce
    Cooking oil, enough to cover bottom of heavy skillet to depth of 1½ inch

Sprinkle cut bananas with sugar, lime juice and rum. Marinate for about an hour. Heat cooking oil to cover in sauce pan. Dip bananas in batter and quickly fry in hot oil, turning only once. Dip in caramel or chocolate as preferred. This recipe is good for about 5 servings.

Van Mullis with Ben and Bill Long

Eddie, Logan, Renee, Punky and Mo Holler

Banana Pudding
Van & Susan Mullis

2 pkgs. instant vanilla pudding mix
3 cups milk
1 cup sour cream
1 (8oz.) ctn. Cool Whip
6 bananas, sliced
Vanilla Wafers

Mix milk with pudding mix and let set for 15 minutes. Add sour cream and Cool Whip to pudding. Layer in a 9x13 dish half of bananas, vanilla wafers, and pudding mixture. Repeat layers.

Refrigerate overnight for best flavor.

Banana Split Dessert
Renee & Ed Holler

½ cup butter or margarine, melted
2 cups graham cracker crumbs
2 eggs
2 cups sifted powdered sugar
1 tsp. vanilla
1 20oz. can crushed pineapple, well drained
4 medium bananas, sliced (about 3 cups)
1 9 oz. carton frozen whipped dessert topping, thawed
½ cup pecans, coarsely chopped
1 4 oz. jar maraschino cherries, drained (1/4 cup)

Combine melted butter or margarine and cracker crumbs. Pat in bottom of 13 ½ x 9 ½ inch pan. Beat eggs on high speed of electric mixer until light about 4 minutes. Add powdered sugar; softened butter and vanilla. Beat 5 minutes. Spread over crumbs. Chill 30 minutes. Spread pineapple over creamed mixture. Arrange bananas over pineapple. Cover with whipped topping. Sprinkle with pecans. Cover and refrigerate 6 hours or overnight. Garnish with cherries.
Makes 12 servings

Desserts

Better Than Sex Cake
Frances Sloan Fulmer

1 pkg. German chocolate cake mix
1 can sweetened condensed milk
1 jar Mrs. Richardson's caramel, butterscotch or fudge
    ice cream topping
1 (8 oz.) Cool Whip

Bake cake as directed on package (9x13 inch pan) and let cool. With a wooden spoon handle, punch holes about one inch over entire cake. Pour whole can of sweet milk into holes. Pour entire jar of topping over cake. Pour entire container of Cool Whip over the topping. Spread grated Heath bar over all.

Blueberry Pound Cake
Sandra & "Big Daddy" Hughes

1 cup plus 2 tbsp. margarine
2/4 cups sugar (divided)
4 eggs
1 tsp. vanilla
3 cups all-purpose flour (divided)
1 tsp. baking powder
½ tsp. salt
2 cups fresh or frozen blueberries

Grease a 10" tube pan with 2 tbsp. butter. Sprinkle pan with the ¼ cup sugar. Cream rest of butter and sugar. Add eggs one at a time, beating well after each one. Add vanilla and mix well. Combine 2 ¾ cups flour, baking powder and salt. Add gradually to creamed mixture. Dredge blueberries with remaining ¼ cup flour. Fold blueberries into batter.

Bake at 350° for 1 hour, 10 minutes (may take longer depending on oven) or until golden brown. Cool in pan for several hours (or overnight) to prevent sticking.

Kay, Van Mullis, Sister Byrum & Sister Mullis

Brittle
Lisa Dievendorf

2 sticks butter
1 cup sugar
Saltine crackers
1 bag semi-sweet chocolate chips
1 cup finely chopped pecans (optional)

Melt sugar and butter in saucepan then boil for 3 minutes. On a cookie sheet, lay out saltine crackers. Pour butter and sugar on top of crackers. Bake in 350° oven for 15 minutes, or watch for bubbles (not too dark). Take out of oven and pour 1 bag of semi-sweet chocolate chips on top. Let sit until chips start to melt. Spread evenly and add nut dust. Place in freezer for 20-30 minutes. Use a knife to break into pieces.

Desserts

Butter Pecan Crunch
Margaret & Tom Price

1 cup butter
1 cup sugar
1 tbsp. light corn syrup
3 tbsp. water
1 (6oz.) pkg. semisweet chocolate chips
1 cup finely chopped pecans

Melt butter in saucepan. Add sugar, syrup and water. Cook; stirring often to hard crack stage (a small amount dropped in water hardens immediately.) Pour onto sheet of wax paper on work surface and use spatula to quickly spread paper thin. Cool for about one hour. Melt chocolate and use spatula to spread over candy. Sprinkle pecans over chocolate. Let dry for several hours, then break into pieces and store in air tight container. Candy is best made on cold, dry winter days as it will require longer to dry in summer. Never make on humid or rainy days. Servings: Makes 20 to 24 pieces.

Candy Bar Pie
Frances Sloan Fulmer

Crust:
    1 ½ cups coconut, grated
    2 tbsp. margarine, melted

Combine coconut and margarine and press into an 8 inch pie pan. Bake at 325° for 10 minutes or until golden brown, Cool.

Filling:
    1 tsp. instant coffee
    2 tbsp. water
    1 bar almond milk chocolate broken into pieces
    4 cups cool-whip, thawed

Melt butter in saucepan. Add sugar, syrup and water. Cook; stirring often to hard crack stage (a small amount dropped in water hardens immediately.) Pour onto sheet of wax paper on work surface and use spatula to quickly spread paper thin. Cool for about one hour. Melt chocolate and use spatula to spread over candy. Sprinkle pecans over chocolate. Let dry for several hours, then break into pieces and store in air tight container. Candy is best made on cold, dry winter days as it will require longer to dry in summer. Never make on humid or rainy days. Servings: Makes 20 to 24 pieces.

Caramel Brownies
Ben & Louise Galloway

1 pkg. light caramels (Kraft)
½ cup evaporated milk
1 pkg. German chocolate cake mix
¾ cup margarine, melted
1/3 cup evaporated milk
1 cup nuts, chopped
1 cup semi-sweet chocolate pieces or morsels

In heavy saucepan combine caramels and ½ cup evaporated milk over very low heat (or microwave) stirring constantly. Set aside melted caramels.

Grease & flour (or Bakers Joy) a 9 x 13 baking pan. Combine cake mix, margarine, 1/3 cup evaporated milk and nuts. Press ½ of the dough into pan. Bake at 350° for 8 minutes.

Sprinkle chocolate pieces over baked crust. Spread caramel mixture over the pieces and crumble the rest of the dough over the caramel layer.

Return to oven and bake for 20-25 minutes. Cool

slightly, then refrigerate about 30 minutes to set caramel layer. Cut like brownies.

I trim the edges of pan off before cutting as they do get a little hard.

Charlotte Russe
Lynn Steedman

This is a dessert that we serve at Thanksgiving and Christmas every year. I was introduced to the tradition by my mother-in-law, Ann Steedman. When she talked about preparing Charlotte Russe, she would always say that she was going to "build" the Charlotte. I think she felt that way because she had to use so many different bowls. I first watched her "build" it, then I helped her "build" it and then it became my responsibility to "build" it. After making Charlotte twice a year for the past 25 years, I feel like I have perfected the process. It took me a while, but now I have the right sequence for "building" this delicious, light and fluffy dessert. It is the perfect ending to a heavy holiday meal. Don't be frightened by the whiskey flavoring…you can add just to taste or leave it out!

    I dozen Lady Fingers
    I pint whipping cream
    3 eggs (separated)
    ¾ cup sugar
    I envelope gelatin
    2-4 tbsp. whiskey
    I tsp. pure vanilla
    I cup whole milk
    Garnish -toasted sliced almonds and maraschino
        cherries

Line the bottom and sides of a triffle bowl with spit lady fingers. Scald the milk, but do not boil. Add gelatin to hot milk and dissolve, set aside and let cool to lukewarm. Beat egg yolks, thoroughly. Add sugar and beat vanilla slowly to cook the egg mixture. While the egg

yolks are beating, in another bowl beat the egg whites until stiff and in another bowl whip the cream until stiff peaks form. When milk/gelatin mixture is lukewarm, pour slowly over egg yolks and then fold in the stiffly beaten egg whites and then add this entire mixture to the whipped cream. Now pour this entire mixture into the bowl lined with Lady Fingers and refrigerate overnight. When ready to serve, Garnish with toasted sliced almonds (cool) and Marischino cherries to taste.

Bill Gambrell
Billy was a three-year football letterman at Carolina and also lettered in track. He played seven years in the NFL with St. Louis Cardinals and Detroit Lions, and played briefly in the Canadian League.

Cheesecake
Jan & Bill Gambrell

    4 pkgs. (8 oz. each) cream cheese, softened
    I ½ cups sugar
    ½ cup cornstarch
    I cup (2sticks) unsalted butter, softened
    2 cups heavy cream
    6 eggs

Pre-heat oven to 350°. Coat a 10 inch spring-form pan with non-stick cooking spray. Wrap outside of the spring-form pan with foil. In a large bowl, beat cream cheese until smooth. Add sugar, then cornstarch, butter, cream, and eggs, beating well after each addition. Pour into prepared spring-form pan. Place in a larger pan filled with 1 inch of water.

(*IMPORTANT: foil should be around spring-form pan in such a way that water does not leak into the spring-form pan!)

Bake at 350° for 1 hour or until dark golden brown. Transfer to a wire rack to cool.

Once Cheesecake has cooled (about 3 hours) remove side of spring-form pan, cover and put in refrigerator. Ready to serve the next day- top with whatever you like or as is!

Servings: 16

weigh down the bread. Set aside for 1 hour to allow the bread to absorb the sauce. (The pudding can be made at this point up to 1 day ahead). Refrigerate.

Heat oven to 325°. Remove the top baking dish and plastic. Bake uncovered 35 to 40 minutes or until set. Serve warm with whipped cream.

To Fake it...and save 1 hour, 10 minutes:
Thaw two 13 oz. packages frozen French toast and cut into 1 ½ inch cubes. Heat oven to 325°. Lightly coat a 13x9 inch baking dish with cooking spray. Place the toast in the dish. Beat 4 cups milk, one 12-oz. can chocolate syrup, and 2 eggs; pour over the toast. Cover with foil and bake 10 minutes. Remove foil and stir. Bake, uncovered, 20 to 25 minutes longer or until set. Serve warm with canned whipped cream.
Serves: 8, with leftovers.

Chocolate Bread Pudding
Linda Flowers

4 cups milk
4 eggs
1/3 cup sugar
8 tbsp. butter or margarine
12 oz. semisweet chocolate chips
1 tsp. vanilla extract
1 loaf white bread, crusts trimmed
1 pint heavy cream, whipped

Whisk the milk, eggs, and sugar in a medium saucepan. Add the butter and chocolate and heat over low heat, stirring only until the butter and chocolate melt. Stir in the vanilla. Lightly coat a 13x9 inch baking dish with cooking spray. Arrange the bread slices in 3 layers. Pour the chocolate sauce over the bread. Cover with plastic wrap and place another baking dish on top to

Chocolate Caramel Pecan Cheesecake
Lucy Hughes

Crust:
2 cups vanilla wafer crumbs
6 tbsp. margarine, melted

Filling:
1 (14 oz.) bag of Kraft caramels
1 (5 oz.) can evaporated milk
2 (8 oz.) pkgs. cream cheese, softened
½ cup sugar
2 eggs
1 cup Baker's real semi-sweet chocolate chips, melted
1 tsp. vanilla flavoring

Preheat oven to 350°. Mix together crumbs and margarine. Press onto bottom and sides of a 9 inch spring form pan. Bake for 10 minutes. In a small bowl, microwave caramels with milk on high for 4-5 minutes or until melted, stirring every minute. Pour over crust. Top with pecans. In a large mixing bowl, beat cream cheese and sugar at medium speed with electric mixer until well blended. Add eggs, mixing well. Blend in chocolate and vanilla. Pour over pecans. Place pan on cookie sheet. Bake for 45 minutes. Loosen cake from rim of pan. Cool before removing rim of pan. Chill for several hours of overnight. Garnish as desired. Preparation time is 35 minutes plus chilling. Baking time is 45 minutes.

Chocolate Chip Cheesecake Ball

Sandra & "Big Daddy" Hughes

1 (8oz. pkg.) Cream Cheese (softened)
½ cup (1 stick) of Butter (softened)
¾ cup powdered sugar
½ tsp. vanilla
¾ cup miniature chocolate chips
Crushed pecans
Chocolate Graham Crackers

Mix cream cheese and butter until smooth. Add in powdered sugar, brown sugar, and vanilla. Mix well. Stir in chocolate chips. Refrigerate for at least two hours. Shape mixture into a ball, wrap in plastic wrap and refrigerate for 1 hour or overnight. Roll cheesecake ball in crushed pecans and serve with chocolate graham crackers.

Prep Wednesday

MARCH 8, 2000 • PAGE C3

BASEBALL | Richland Northeast's Derrick Grantz and Clay Mitchell

Grantz & Mitchell

Derrick Grantz and Clay Mitchell are outstanding baseball players in their senior year at Richland Northeast High School. And that's where the comparison only starts.

They were born within one month of each other. They both played football until their junior year. They both have been closest friends since birth. Both had fathers that were football stars at the University of South Carolina whose names are in the program's record books.

Clay's father, Jimmy, was an All-Atlantic Coast Conference receiver at USC from 1969-71, who ranks 13th on the Gamecocks all-time reception list. Jimmy was a graduate assistant in 1972, the year Jeff Grantz arrived. Derrick's father, Jeff, was an All-American quarterback at Carolina. In a *State* paper poll two years ago, he was voted the best quarterback in the history of Gamecock football. Jeff and Jimmy were in each other's weddings.

The two families compete with one another like bitter enemies. Derrick and Clay compare test scores

Desserts

and batting averages, and Jeff and Jimmy compete on the golf course.

Chocolate Eclair Cake
Ruth Grantz

Use a 9x13 dish
2 small pkgs. of French Vanilla Instant Pudding
3 cups cold milk
1 8 oz. tub of Cool Whip
Butter
Graham Crackers (do not crush)

Beat together for two minutes the instant pudding and milk. Fold in cool whip. Butter 9x13 dish. Line bottom with graham crackers. Add layer of pudding mix and another layer of graham crackers—second layer of pudding mix and finish with third layer of crackers.

Topping:
  2 squares unsweetened chocolate
  3 tbsp. butter
  2 tbsp. Karo syrup
  1 tbsp. vanilla
  1 ½ cups confectioners (xxxx) sugar
  3 tbsp. milk

Melt together over low heat chocolate and butter. Remove from heat and add Karo syrup, vanilla, sugar and milk. Spread on top of graham crackers.
Refrigerate 24 hours.
Servings: 15

Chocolate Pound Cake
Mary Hughes

 2 sticks butter
¼ tsp. baking powder
1/4 cup shortening

¼ tsp. salt
1 box confectioners' sugar
½ cup cocoa
5 eggs
1 cup milk
3 cups cake flour
2 tsp. vanilla

Cream butter and shortening, add sugar and cream. Add eggs, one at a time – beat well. Mix dry ingredients and sift 3 times. Add milk and dry ingredients to mixture alternately. Blend in flavoring and mix well. Bake in preheated oven at 300° for about 2 hours.

Coconut Cake
Pauline & Eric Hyman

Cook one box of Duncan Hines Butter Recipe Cake. *Cook in 3 layers according to directions on box. It has to be this brand and use* real butter.

While cake is baking, mix the following: 2 cups sour cream, 2 cups sugar. *Add* 2 pkg. of frozen coconut (thawed enough to break up and mix in above mixture). *Fold in* one 12 oz. container of Cool Whip (original, not creamy) *Put this mixture in refrigerator while cake is cooling.*

Ice each layer generously to where it oozes over the sizes. Then ice the whole cake. If the icing is too runny add more whip cream to "thicken" it. Typically letting it "set" in refrigerator while cake cools thickens it up. Sprinkle some flake coconut (Angel Flake from a can) on top of cake for "effect". You may have a little icing left over.

The cake then goes in a sealed Tupperware cake plate/ cover and sets for three days in the refrigerator. This is important!! The cake mellows and taste better each day after the three days, but if you eat before three days, it's not as good.

Coconut Squares
Vann & Susan Mullis

½ cut butter
1/2 cup brown sugar
1 cup flour

Mix and put into 8x10 dish. Bake 10 minutes at 375°. Then mix together the following ingredients:

1 cup brown sugar
2 eggs
1 tsp. vanilla
1 ½ cups coconut
3 tbsp. flour
½ tsp. salt
1 cup nuts, chopped

Pour over first mixture and return to oven for 20 minutes. Cool and cut in squares.

Colin's Pinto Beans Geechie Pie
Colin Ayers

3 eggs
2 sticks of butter (microwave)
3 cups sugar
1 cup pecans, chopped
1 cup coconut, shredded
1 can pinto beans, drained and mashed up
1 shot of Jack Daniel's

Mix all the above ingredients and put in two prepared pie crust. Cook at 350° for 35 minutes.

Charlie, Alex & Howard Hughes

Cream Cheese Lemon Squares
Sandra & Howard Hughes

box lemon cake mix
1 egg
1 stick margarine (melted)

Mix together these three ingredients and press in the bottom of a glass 9x13 casserole dish. Next, mix the following ingredients and pour over the bottom layer (I don't even wash out the bowl from the first three items):

- 1 8-oz. bar cream cheese (softened, room temperature)
- 2 eggs
- 1 box 10X powdered sugar

When mixed, it may appear lumpy, but that's okay. The cream cheese melts in the oven while cooking. Bake at 350° for approximately 40 minutes or until golden brown on top. Let cool completely before cutting. They must be completely cold. I usually bake at night and let sit overnight or bake early in the morning and let sit all day before cutting.

J.R. Wilburn

J.R. was the Gamecocks' leading receiver in 1964 and 1965. He was also outstanding in track. He was drafted by the Pittsburgh Steelers and played there for five seasons.

Cream Cheese-Topped Pineapple Cake
J.R. Wilburn
Submitted by Alfred Johnson

- 2 eggs
- 2 cups sugar
- 2 cups all purpose flour
- 1 20 oz. can crushed pineapple packed in its own juice, undrained
- ½ cup pecans, chopped
- 2 tsp. baking soda
- 1 tsp. vanilla

Cream Cheese Frosting:
- 2 cups powdered sugar
- 1 9 oz. pkg. cream cheese, room temperature
- ¼ cup (1/2 stick) butter, room temperature
- 1 tsp. vanilla

Preheat oven to 350°. Lightly grease 9x13 baking pan. Beat eggs in large bowl until light and fluffy. Add sugar and continue beating until thick. Stir in flour, pineapple, pecans, baking soda and vanilla and mix thoroughly. Pour batter into prepared pan. Bake until tester inserted in center comes out clean, about 40 to 45 minutes. Let cake cool in pan on rack.

Sprinkle nuts decoratively over cake. Cut into squares. Serve cake at room temperature.

Cream Pound Cake
Orral Anne & Jim Moss

- 2 sticks butter, leave out to soften
- 3 cups sugar,
- 6 eggs, room temperature
- 3 cups plain unbleached flour
- 1 cup heavy whipping cream (do not whip)
- 1 tsp. vanilla extract
- ½ tsp. almond extract
- ½ tsp. lemon extract

Mix butter and sugar in a mixer and add eggs one at a time. Blend in the flour and cream and then the extracts. Grease and flour bunt pan or tube pan and put in oven and turn on to 325° for 1 hour and 20 minutes. Delicious!

Debbie's Banana & Oreo Surprise
Debbie Faulk

15 Oreo cookies, crushed
3 bananas
Pecans
Chocolate syrup
1 pt. whipping cream
Sugar (for whipping cream)
Strawberries

Layer crushed Oreo cookies. Add banana, dribble syrup and then add whipped cream over entire top. Refrigerate for at least a couple of hours. It gets better the longer it is refrigerated. (You can add almost anything to this, such as blueberries, cherries etc.)

Dreama's Fruit Cake
Dreama Sue Osborne

4 cups of plain flour
4 eggs
2 cups sugar
½ lb. margarine
2 tsp. soda
2 lbs. candied fruit
1 pint of strawberry preserves
1 8 oz. box of pitted prunes
1 box of white raisins
1 can of applesauce
1 tsp. each of cinnamon, nutmeg, allspice and cloves
1 lb. of English walnuts
½ lb. black walnuts

Mix well and bake at 250° for 3 to 3 ½ hours. This recipe will make two cakes. (This is nice to do at Christmas, one for home and one for friends.)

Desserts

Dreama's Old Timey Sweets
Dreama Sue Osborne

This tastes just like the old timey kind and is great for tailgating.

I box 10X powdered sugar
I stick margarine
¼ cup carnation milk
½ cup Hershey's cocoa
Dash of salt

Mix all together and microwave on high heat two minutes. Take out and add ¾ cup pecans, stir well and microwave another minute. Stir well and pour into a buttered container. Let cool and then cut into squares and you are ready for the game.

Dump Cake
Frances Sloan Fulmer

Layer ingredients in 9x13 inch pan in order. DO NOT STIR.
  I can cherry pie filling
  I can crushed pineapple and juice
  I yellow cake mix (sprinkle box)
  I cup nuts
  2 sticks margarine (sliced up)

Bake I hour at 350°. Serve warm with Cool Whip. Garnish with cherries.

Easy Banana Pudding
Betsy Collins

I box instant vanilla pudding, prepared
I container Cool Whip
Vanilla wafers
Bananas cut up

Mix together prepared vanilla pudding and Cool Whip. Alternate layers of vanilla wafers, bananas, and pudding/ Cool Whip mixture.

Refrigerate until chilled and ready to serve. So simple and easy!

Easy Egg Custard Pie
Al Johnson

4 eggs
I ½ cups sugar
½ cup self-rising flour
2 cups milk
I ½ tsp. vanilla
½ stick butter, melted

Beat eggs, Blend in sugar and flour. Add remaining ingredients. Pour into greased pie pan, and place on a cookie sheet. Bake at 350° for 40 minutes or until knife comes out clean.

Note: This easy pie forms its own crust.

English Toffee
Margaret & Tom Price

2 cups butter
2 cups sugar
2 tbsp. water
12 oz chocolate chips
1 cup pecans, finely chopped

Combine butter, sugar and water in large heavy bottom saucepan. Heat; stir constantly until mixture is a deep caramel color. Pour into a greased 15x10 inch jelly roll pan. Sprinkle with chips and spread when melted. Sprinkle with nuts. Cool completely. Break into pieces.
Servings: Yields 70 pieces.

Gamecock Brittle
Debbie Faulk

1 stick of butter
1 stick margarine
½ cup sugar
1 lb. pecans, broken up
Graham crackers

Line a bread pan with foil with sides up a little. Layer graham crackers (whole) side by side. Cover graham crackers with the pecans. Boil the butter, margarine and sugar for 2 minutes. Pour over the pecans. Bake in preheated oven 17 to 18 minutes @ 350°. Let cool and break into pieces.

Sonny Edwards

Gloria's Blueberry Pie
Sonny & Martha Ruth Edwards

Spray 10x6x2 or 8x11x2 casserole with cooking spray.

3 cups blueberries
1 tbsp. lemon juice drizzled over fruit
Mix 1 1/2 cups sugar,
1 egg beaten,
1 cup Bisquick

Stir until coarse like meal; sprinkle over top of fruit. Drizzle ¼ stick plus 2 tablespoons of margarine over top. Bake at 400° for 30 minutes.
For peach or apple pie, omit blueberries and add 3 cups peaches or 3 cups of apples. Also add 1 tablespoon cornstarch and ¼ cup light brown sugar stirred into ½ cup water.

Desserts

Heath Bar Cake
Andrea Bailey
Submitted by Stuart Whatley

I used to make this with Heath Bars, but they are hard to find now. So I substitute toffee crunch bits and milk chocolate chips.

 2 cups flour
 1 cup brown sugar
 ½ cup sugar
 ½ cup oil

Mix in large bowl, take out ½ to 1 cup and save for topping. Then add to remaining mixture
 1 cup sour milk (milk plus 1 tbsp. vinegar)
 1 egg
 1 tsp. vanilla
 1 tsp. soda

Mix well, pour into greased 9x12 pan. Top with 6 to 8 crushed Heath bars (or toffee crunch and milk chocolate chips). 1 cup chopped pecans and the remaining crumb mixture. Bake at 350° for about 30-40 minutes.

Huguenot Torte
Margaret & Ruddy Attaberry

 1 ½ cups apples, peeled & chopped
 3 eggs
 2 ¼ cups sugar
 3 ¾ tsp. baking powder
 ¾ tsp. salt
 7 tbsp. flour
 1 tsp. vanilla
 1 ½ cups pecans, chopped

Peel and cut up apples, soak in lemon juice. In a mixing bowl, beat eggs until lemon colored. Add sugar, mix, and then add baking powder, salt and flour. Blend well. Add vanilla and fold in drained apples and pecans. Pour into a well greased 9x11 pan. Bake at 350° for about 45 minutes until crust is brown.

Cut into squares and serve topped with sherry flavored whipping cream.

Lemon Cookies
Frances Sloan Fulmer

 1 box Duncan Hines Lemon Supreme Cake Mix
 4 ½ oz. (small size) Cool Whip
 2 eggs
 10x confectioners sugar

Beat eggs until light. Add cake mix and cool whip. Mix thoroughly. Roll the batter in sifted sugar using 2 forks. Slice cookies and put on greased cookie sheets about 1 ½ to 2 inches apart. Bake at 350° until lightly browned (do not over bake) about 9 or 10 minutes. Cool on wire racks.
Makes about 6 dozen cookies about 2 inches in diameter.

Lemon Jell-O Pound Cake
Emily White

 1 (18 ¼ oz.) Package Yellow Cake Mix (the kind with pudding in the mix)
 1 (3 oz.) Package Lemon Jell-O
 ¾ cup water
 1 tsp. Lemon Flavoring
 ¾ cup Vegetable Oil
 4 eggs

Grease and flour a 10-inch tube cake pan. Preheat oven to 350°.

Add dry Jell-O to dry cake mix and blend well. Add ¾ cup of water, the lemon flavoring, vegetable oil and eggs (add one egg at a time and blend well after each addition).

Pour batter in pan, bake for 45 minutes or until a toothpick inserted in the cake comes out clean. Allow cake to cool in pan about 15 minutes before removing.
Servings: 4

Little Cheesecakes
Pam Harrison

2 8 oz. pkgs. cream cheese
2 eggs
¾ cup sugar
1 tsp. vanilla
1 tbsp. lemon juice
1 can cherry pie filling

Beat all ingredients except pie filling and wafers together until smooth and fluffy. Line muffin pans with cupcake liners and place vanilla wafers in bottom of liner. Fill one half full with cream cheese mixture. Bake at 375° for 15 to 20 minutes. Do not brown. They will start to crack when done. Cool thoroughly and put filling on top.

I use mini muffin pans and bit size vanilla wafers (I find them at Kroger).
Makes 24 regular or 48 small.

Lusious Lemon Pie
Kathi & Jimmy Mitchell

1 pkg. instant vanilla pudding mix
1 small can frozen lemonade, thawed
12 oz. carton Cool Whip
1 ¾ cups milk
1 Oreo pie crust

Prepare instant pudding using milk. Stir in lemonade, mix well. Fold in Cool Whip. Pour into pie crust. Freeze until firm. When ready to serve, let stand at room temperature for about 5 minutes. Garnish with a dollop of Cool Whip, if desired.

David Byrum & Van Mullis

Marion's Apple Pie
Vann & Susan Mullis

Thaw and crumble Mrs. Smith's Apple Crumb Pie in 9x12 pan. Melt 1 stick of butter with ½ cup brown sugar and ½ cup nuts. Pour over top of pie.
Bake at 350° for 35 to 45 minutes.

Desserts

Melt in Your Mouth Pecan Pie
Margaret & Tom Price

1 ½ cups sugar
1 tbsp. all purpose flour
4 eggs
¾ cup light corn syrup
1 tbsp. butter, melted
2 tsp. vanilla
1 ½ cups pecans, chopped
1 unbaked 9-inch pastry shell

Combine sugar, flour, eggs, syrup, butter, vanilla and pecans. Pour filling into pastry shell. Bake at 325° for 50 to 55 minutes or until firm at center.
Servings: 8

Million Dollar Pound Cake
Debbie & Durry Faulk

For the best results, preheat your oven to 300° before you begin. Also soften butter at room temperature for 30 minutes. I also put out my eggs and milk.

1 pound butter, softened
3 cups sugar
6 large eggs
4 cups all-purpose flour
¾ cup milk
1 tsp. almond extract
1 tsp. vanilla extract

Beat butter at medium speed with an electric mixer until creamy. (The butter will become a lighter yellow color; this is an important step, as the job of the mixer is to incorporate air into the butter so the cake will rise. It will take 1 to 17 minutes, depending on the power of your mixer.) Gradually add sugar, beating at medium speed until light and fluffy. (Again, the times will vary, and butter will turn to a fluffy white.) Add eggs, 1 at a time, beating just until yellow yolk disappears.

Add flour to creamed mixture alternately with milk, beginning and ending with flour. Beat at low speed just until blended after each addition. (The batter should be smooth and bits of flour should be well incorporated: to rid batter of lumps, stir gently with rubber spatula.) Stir in extracts.

Pour into a greased and floured 10-inch tube pan. (Spray with Baker's Joy with flour, or use old way of greased and floured pan. Be sure to get every nook and cranny covered).

Bake at 300° for 1 hour and 40 minutes or until a long wooded pick inserted in center comes out clean. Cool in pan on a wire rack 10 to 15 minutes. Remove from pan.

Mitchell's Mocha Cheesecake
Kathi & Jimmy Mitchell

½ cup chocolate wafer crumbs
¼ cup sugar
½ cup butter, melted
1 8 oz. package cream cheese, softened
14 oz. sweetened condensed milk
2 tbsp. instant coffee granules
1 tbsp. hot water
2/3 cup chocolate syrup
1 cup whipping cream, whipped

Combine first three ingredients; press into an 8-inch spring form pan. Chill.

Beat cream cheese at medium speed with an electric mixer until fluffy; add unsweetened condensed

milk, beating well. Dissolve coffee granules in 1 tbsp. hot water. Add coffee and chocolate syrup to cream cheese mixture, beating well. Fold in whipped cream. Spoon into prepared crust. Freeze 6 hours.
Serves 6 to 8

My Mother's Pound Cake
Cathy Hughes
Publisher of The Times and Democrat

If you bake this cake for a tailgate, you won't have to worry about bringing any home.

2 sticks butter
1 stick margarine
2/3 cuts sugar
2/3 cups cake flour
6 eggs
Juice of lemon

Cream together the butter, margarine and sugar with an electric mixer. Sift the flour and add to the the batter half at a time, alternating with the eggs, and ending with the lemon juice.

Grease and flour a tube pan; cut waxed paper to line the bottom, then grease and flour the paper as well.

Bake in a pre-heated 350-degree oven for approximately 50 minutes or until the sides start separating from the edges of the pan and the top is golden brown. Loosen the edges with a knife and remove from the pan immediately.

Pecan Pralines
Margaret & Tom Price

2 cups sugar
1 cup firmly packed brown sugar
3/4 cup whipping cream
2 tbsp. butter
1 tsp. vanilla
4 cups pecans

Combine sugar, brown sugar and cream in saucepan. Bring to boil and cook for 3 minutes. Stir in butter, vanilla and pecans. Drop mixture by tablespoonful to form 1 ½ inch pralines on aluminum foil or wax paper sheet, adding cream if mixture thickens too quickly.
Servings: 18 to 24

Plantation Pecan Crunch
Margaret & Tom Price

2 cups butter
2 cups sugar
½ tsp. salt
¼ cup water
2 tbsp. corn syrup
1 (6 oz.) pkg. semisweet chocolate chips
2 cups finely chopped toasted pecans

Melt butter in heavy saucepan. Add sugar and cook, stirring constantly, until dissolved; do not burn. Add salt, water and syrup. Cook to brittle stage or to register 200° on candy thermometer, stirring constantly. Remove from heat and pour into 2 shallow pans, spreading evenly to a thin layer. While candy cools, melt chocolate chips in top of double boiler over hot water. Spread chocolate on candy layer and sprinkle

Desserts

with pecans. Let stand to cool, and then break into pieces like peanut brittle.
Servings: Makes 25 to 30 pieces.

Pralines
Margaret & Tom Price

3 cups sugar divided
1 cup whole milk
2 cups pecan halves

Combine two cups sugar with milk in a large heavy saucepan. Brown the remaining cup of sugar in a non-stick saucepan until caramel colored. Bring milk mixture to a slow boil. Add caramelized sugar. Cook to a soft ball stage (238°) and add nuts. Remove from heat and beat, and beat, and beat until thickened. Drop by spoonfuls onto wax paper and let harden.
Servings: Yields two dozen

Punch Bowl Cake
Ria & Edwin Floyd

1 Box 4X (xxxx) confectioners sugar
1 small can evaporated milk
1 sour cream (2 cups)
1 large Cool Whip
1 Angle food cake
2 boxes frozen strawberries, I used fresh strawberries
1 jar of strawberry glaze

In large bowl, tear Angle food cake in small pieces- put in bowl, while thawing strawberries. Mix sugar and milk until mixed well. Add sour cream and cool whip by folding in lightly. Pour over cake and toss lightly. Mix thawed or fresh strawberries and glaze and put this mixture over all. Chill.

You will need a large bowl for this. It will serve 25 people.

Quick and Easy Cheesecake
Susan Hughes

1 cup graham cracker crumbs
3 tbsp. sugar
1 tbsp. margarine, melted
3 8-oz. pkgs. cream cheese, softened
¾ cup sugar
3 eggs
1 cup mini semi-sweet chocolate chips
1 tsp. vanilla flavoring

Combine crumbs, sugar and margarine; press onto bottom of 9-inch spring form pan. Combine cream cheese and sugar, mixing at medium speed on electric mixer until well blended. Add eggs, one at a time, mixing well after each addition. Blend in chocolate pieces and vanilla; pour over crust. Bake at 450° for 10 minutes. Reduce oven temperature to 250°; continue baking 35 minutes. Loosen cake from rim of pan; cool before removing rim of pan. Chill before serving.

Mary Kay & Chip Wilson

Rice Crispy Peanut Butter-M&M Treats
Mary Kay & Chip Wilson

3 cups Crispy Rice cereal, Kellogg's Rice Krispies
1 cup of extra crunchy peanut butter
1 cup of peanut butter chips, Reese's
1 jar (7oz.) Marshmallow Crème, Kraft puffed
½ cup of miniature M&M's

Line cookie sheet with waxed paper. Using two wooden spoons toss rice cereal, peanut butter, peanut butter chips, and miniature M&M's in a large bowl to coat. Add Marshmallow Crème and toss until well combined.

Using an ice cream scoop form mixture into 1 ½ inch balls. Place on prepared cookie sheet. Refrigerate for 1 hour or until firm. Store in airtight container.

Ruby Slipper Cake
Cheryl Wheat

1 box yellow cake mix with pudding included in mix
1 cup sour cream
¼ cup water
2 eggs
1 pkg. (3oz.) Jell-O brand raspberry gelatin

Combine cake mix, sour cream, water and eggs in large bowl. Blend, then at medium speed, beat for 2 minutes, until creamy. Spoon 1/3 of batter into well-greased and floured Bundt pan. Sprinkle with ½ the gelatin. Repeat layers. Spread remaining batter over gelatin to cover. (Avoid getting gelatin on sides of pan, it will stick.)

Bake at 350° for 45 to 50 minutes until cake springs back when touched. Cool in pan 5 minutes. Remove and cool on rack. Sprinkle with confectioners sugar. Tastes like jelly cake. This recipe was given to me by Grace Calloway, Milledgeville, Ga.

Skillet Pineapple Upside Down Cake
Pam & Pete Minaya

Pete's favorite Southern Cake.
    ¼ cup butter
    2/3 cup firmly packed light or dark brown sugar
    1 (20 oz.) can pineapple slices, undrained
    9 maraschino cherries
    2 large eggs, separated
    ¾ cup granulated sugar
    ¾ cup all-purpose flour
    1/8 tsp. salt
    ½ tsp. baking power

Desserts

Melt butter in a 9-inch cast-iron skillet. Spread brown sugar evenly over bottom of skillet. Drain pineapple, reserving ¼ cup juice; set juice aside. Arrange pineapple slices in a single layer over brown sugar mixture, and place a cherry in center of each pineapple ring; set skillet aside.

Beat egg yolks at medium speed with an electric mixer until thick and lemon-colored; gradually add granulated sugar, beating well.

Heat reserved pineapple juice in a small saucepan over low heat. Gradually add juice mixture to the yolk mixture, beating until blended.

Combine all-purpose flour, salt, and baking powder; add dry ingredients to the yolk mixture, beating at low speed with electric mixer until blended.

Beat egg whites until stiff peaks form; fold egg whites into batter. Spoon batter evenly over pineapple slices. Bake at 325° for 45 to 50 minutes. Cool cake in skillet 30 minutes; invert cake onto a serving plate. Serve warm or cold.

Strawberry Cake
LTC Alfred Johnson, USMC (retired)

1 box Duncan Hines strawberry supreme cake mix
2 tbsp. flour
1 pkg. strawberry jello (family size)
1 cup Wesson oil
½ cup water
4 eggs
¾ cup frozen strawberries, thawed

Blend well. Bake in 3 layer cake pans at 350° for about 20 minutes.

ICING:
1 ½ sticks butter, softened
1 ½ boxes 4X confectioners sugar
½ cup frozen strawberries, thawed

Sweet Tea Pie
Frank Beatty

This recipe comes from Martha Foose, owner of the Mockingbird Bakery in Greenwood, MS. IT IS AWESOME!

Crust:
2 cups flour, White Lilly all-purpose preferred (use 1 ½ cups of flour and ½ cup of cake flour if not using
White Lilly)
1 tsp. salt
1 tsp. sugar
½ tbsp (1 ½ sticks) unsalted butter, cold and cut into pieces
¼ cup shortening or lard, cold and cut into pieces

In a food processor, combine flour, salt and sugar. Pulse once or twice. Add butter and pulse several times. Add the shortening and pulse until no piece is bigger than a black-eyed-pea and the ingredients look like a course meal (called shaggy dough). Pour out on table, take egg-size piece and smear them on the table. Gather up all the smears and form into a disc. Wrap in plastic and place in freezer for 10 minutes.

Remove dough and roll or press into a 9-inch regular pie place. Keep cold while making the filing.

Filling:
1 cup (2 sticks) unsalted butter at room temperature
2 cups sugar
Zest of 1 lemon, grated
8 large egg yolks

2/3 cup strongly brewed black tea (try orange pekoe)
1 tbsp. vanilla
½ tsp. freshly squeezed lemon juice
½ tsp. apple cider vinegar
2 tbls. flour
2 tsp. cornmeal
Lemon peel and mint leaves as optional garnish

Preheat oven to 350°.

In a stand mixer, cream together butter, sugar and lemon zest until light and yellow. Add egg yolks one at a time, mixing a second or two after each addition. With mixer running on low speed, add tea, vanilla, lemon juice and vinegar. Mix in flour and cornmeal. Pour into crust.

Bake for 40 minutes, or until slightly bubbly and almost set. Cool at room temperature for at least 2 hours before serving. If serving later, cover with plastic wrap and refrigerate. Can be made up to 2 days in advance. Garnish with candied lemon peel and mint leaves as desired.

Dessarts

Charlie

Bacon Wrapped Sirloin Roast - Charlie

Beurre Blance - Charlie

Blackberry Cobbler - Charlie

Charleston Pudding - Charlie

Chicken Pot Pie - Charlie

Cilantro Snapper with Salsa Served Atop Grits - Charlie

Gourmet Baked Chicken - Charlie

Gourmet Crown of Lamb with Rosemary - Charlie

Gourmet Stuffing Mushrooms - Charlie

Herbed Encrusted Grouper - Charlie

Herbed New Potatoes - Charlie

Parmigiano Regiano Crusted Port Tenderloin - Charlie

Petites Pois - Charlie

Pork Chops with Caramelized Onions - Charlie

Roast Pork with Rosemary - Charlie

Scalloped Potatoes with Sweet Vidalia Onions - Charlie

Seasoned Rice Pilaf - Charlie

Smothered Chicken Breast - Charlie

Southern Fried Catfish - Charlie

Spicy Aioli - Charlie

Spinach Dip - Charlie

Strawberry Dessert - Charlie

Bacon Wrapped Sirloin Roast
Charlie

2 to 2 ½ lbs. tip sirloin roast, boned, tied
2 to 3 tbsp. Dijon-style mustard
½ tsp. dried thyme leaves
6 slices bacon
4 medium onions cut into wedges
Cherry tomatoes or tomato wedges, for garnish

Cut a few slits on top of roast for bacon drippings to penetrate the meat. Spread mustard evenly over top and sides of roast. Sprinkle with thyme leaves. Place roast on rack in baking pan. Cover tightly with bacon slices, wrapping them around meat.

Bake meat at 325° until a meat thermometer registers 160° for medium rare. Cooking time is about 1 ½ hours. Check for doneness with a fork. Juices should run slightly pink for medium rare. Add onions 40 minutes before roast is expected to be ready.

Remove roast to carving board. Let rest covered for at least 15 minutes before slicing. Slice meat into even slices. Serve with onions, bacon slices, if desired and gravy made from pan drippings. Bacon gets crispy when cooking with roast.

Garnish with cherry tomatoes or tomato wedges.

Beurre Blanc
Charlie

This is a sauce to be serve with grilled or pan fried grouper.

2 tsp. minced shallot
1/3 cup white wine
Salt and ground black pepper, to taste
1 stick cold butter, cubed

Combine first 3 ingredients in a small saucepan over medium heat. Continue cooking and stir occasionally until reduced to a couple of tablespoons, about 5 minutes. Cool for 2 minutes. Turn the heat back on as low as possible and add the butter, One cube at a time, stirring each piece in until it is melted and incorporated. When the sauce is creamy and smooth and all the butter has been incorporated, the sauce is ready to serve.

Blackberry Cobbler
Charlie

8 tbsp. (1 stick) unsalted butter
4 cups blackberries, washed
1 cup sugar
1 cup all-purpose flour
2 tsp. baking powder
Pinch of salt
1 cup milk
1 tsp. pure vanilla extract
Vanilla ice cream, for serving

Place butter in a large oven proof casserole dish or cast iron pan and place in a cold oven. Heat the oven to 350 degrees. Using a large bowl, toss blackberries with 3 tablespoons sugar, set aside. Using a medium bowl, sift together flour, baking powder and salt.

Once the oven has reached 350° remove pan from oven. Pour batter into pan, pour blackberries and any accumulated juices into the center of the batter. Bake until a cake tester inserted into batter comes out clean and top is golden brown, about 1 hour. Serve warm with vanilla ice cream.

Charleston Pudding
Charlie

This southern dessert has a texture between a sticky cake and bread pudding. Use a combination of Fuji and McIntosh apples.

    2 cups peeled, cored, and coarsely chopped tart apples
        (about 2 medium)
    1 tbsp Apple Brandy
    ¼ cup all-purpose flour
    2 tsp. baking powder
    1/8 tsp. salt
    1 cup packed brown sugar
    1 tsp. vanilla extract
    2 large eggs
    1/3 cup chopped pecans, toasted
    Cooking spray.

Preheat oven to 350°. Combine apple and brandy tossing well to coat. Lightly spoon flour into dry measuring cup, level with knife or flat object. Combine Flour, baking powder and salt in a medium bowl, mix well.

Place sugar, vanilla, and eggs in a large bowl, beat with a mixer at medium speed 3 minutes or until thick. With mixer on low speed, gradually add flour mixture.

Gently fold in apple mixture and pecans. Spoon batter into an 8 inch square baking pan coated with cooking spray.

Bake at 350° for 25 minutes or until top is puffed and deep golden brown.
Serve warm.
Yield: 6 servings

Chicken Pot Pie
Charlie

    1 whole chicken, skinned and boned
    2 potatoes, peeled and cubed small
    2 carrots, pared and sliced ¼ inch thick
    1 onion, cut into 8's
    1 small can of English peas
    ¼ tsp. tarragon
    1 tbsp. fresh parsley, chopped
    4 tbsp. butter
    3 cups chicken broth (from cooking chicken)
    3 tbsp. flour
    2 boiled eggs, chopped fine
    Dash of paprika
    Dash of Lawry's seasoning salt
    Dash of Mrs. Dash
    Few drops of Worcestershire sauce
    Ready to use pie dough

Cook chicken on low about 1 hour. Remove chicken to cool. Take chicken broth and cover the vegetables and cook until tender with seasonings and 1 tbsp. of butter.

In another pan heat 3 tbsp. butter. When bubbly, add flour and mix well. Cook for about 2 minutes, stirring. Stir in juice you cooked the veggies in. This will become thick. Add eggs. Might need some more broth, you be the judge of that.

Preheat oven to 350°. Put chicken and veggies in a deep casserole dish and pour sauce over. Cover with pie dough. Score the dough so steam can escape. Cook for about 45 minutes or until dough is golden brown.

I serve jelled cranberry sauce or sliced pineapple with the pie.

Charlie

145

Cilantro Snapper with Salsa Served Atop Grits
Charlie

2 tbs. olive oil
6 (6-8 oz.) snapper filets
2 cups olive oil
4 tbs. blackened or Cajun seasoning
Juice from 1 ½ lemons
½ cup white wine
2 tbs. Worcestershire sauce
¼ tsp. cayenne pepper

GRITS:
2 ½ cups yellow stone-ground grits
¾ cup onion, diced
¾ cup pancetta (or bacon)
9 cups chicken stock
1 cup heavy cream
Salt and pepper to taste
2 cups Parmesan cheese, shredded

SALSA:
3 large vine ripe tomatoes, diced
¾ cup onion, diced
1 cup green and red bell pepper, diced
1 ¼ fresh cilantro, chopped
1 cup tomato juice
Juice of 2 limes
1 tbs. ground cumin
1 tbs. ground coriander
¼ tsp. cayenne

For Snapper:
Mix 2 cups olive oil, blackened seasoning, lemon juice, white wine, Worcestershire and ¼ tsp. cayenne pepper. Whisk to blend well. Pour over snapper filets and refrigerate at least 2 hours or overnight. In a large skillet, heat 2 tbs. olive oil. Add snapper with a little of the marinade and sauté until done.

For Grits:
In a large pot, sauté bacon and onion and onion with a little bit of olive oil. Add chicken stock and cream; bring to a simmer. Add grits, stirring constantly to prevent lumps. Add salt and pepper. When grits come to a nice consistency, add Parmesan cheese and then thyme.

For Salsa:
Combine tomatoes, onions, peppers and cilantro in a bowl; mix well. Then add tomato juice, lime juice and seasonings; mix well.

To serve divide grits evenly among 6 plates. Place 1 snapper filet in center of grits. Top with a spoonful of salsa and serve with spinach or collard greens that has been sautéed in butter.

Gourmet Baked Chicken
Charlie

8 skinless, boneless chicken breast *
1 stick butter
1 clove garlic, finely minced
Monterey Jack and Colby cheese
Parmesan cheese
Minced parsley
½ cup White wine
Panko*
Lawry's seasoning salt
Mrs. Dash seasoning, original blend

Lightly salt and pepper chicken breast and coat evenly with mixture of panko and parmesan cheese. Sauté in butter and garlic mixture. Put browned chicken pieces in a baking pan. Garnish each piece with minced parsley and a slice of cheese. Pour ½ cup of wine over chicken and bake uncovered for 30 minutes at 350°.

 * Panko is a Japanese bread crumb that I use all the time. Look for it in your favorite grocery store or on-line.

Charlie TIP: I skin and debone my own chicken breast. It seems to be moister.

Gourmet Crown of Lamb with Rosemary
Charlie

I lean crown roast of lamb with 14 chops (two 7-rib racks of lamb tied)
¼ cup chopped fresh rosemary
12 garlic cloves, minced
2 tbls. fresh oregano, chopped
I tbl. salt
2 tsp. black pepper
2 ½ tbls. extra-virgin olive oil
Fresh parsley (for garnish)

Preheat oven to 450°. Mix rosemary, garlic, oregano, salt and pepper in small bowl.

Place lamb on large baking sheet and brush with olive oil. Rub herbs on lamb. Cover bones loosely with sheet of foil and roast until an instant thermometer inserted into thickest part of lamb registers 125 to 130° (about 20 minutes) 130 to 135° for medium-rare (about 30 minutes) 140° for medium (about 35 minutes). I like Lamb cooked rare to medium rare.

Transfer lamb to platter and let stand, 5 to 10 minutes. Remove foil. Cut lamb between ribs into chops and serve on a bed of parsley.

Gourmet Stuffed Potatoes
Charlie

4 large baking potatoes
4 oz. crumbled bleu cheese
I bunch scallions or green onions, chopped
¼ cup heavy cream
½ lb. bacon, cooked, drained and chopped

Bake potatoes in 375° oven until done. Remove from oven and allow to cool. Cut off ¼ of each potato lengthwise. Using spoon, scoop the meat of each potato out of the skins and lids, being careful not to damage the skins. Discard the lids. Place meat of potatoes in mixing bowl with all other ingredients and mix well, be careful not to mix too long or the glutens in the potatoes will activate and the mix will become gooey. Replace mixture into each potato skin shell with a spoon.

Bake potatoes in oven at 350° until cheese melts and serve.

Gourmet Stuffing Mushrooms
Charlie

I2 large mushrooms
I lb. sausage
½ cup Italian seasoned bread crumbs
1/3 cup chopped red bell peppers
1/3 cup finely minced onion
4 tbls. chopped fresh sage, or 2 tbls. dried sage

Pop stems from mushroom caps. Preheat oven to 350°. In a mixing bowl, blend sausage, bread crumbs, sage and red peppers, and onions if desired. Wetting hands with cold water will keep sausage mixture from sticking to your hands and make it easier to form small 1-1 ½ inch balls.

Place sausage balls into the mushroom cap and place on an ungreased cookie sheet. Place in the oven at 325° for 30 to 45 minutes.

Mushrooms will loose moisture; however, they will re-absorb flavor and moisture from the sausage. Once done, remove and blot the bottoms of the mushrooms on paper towels and place on a serving platter garnished with parsley. Superior flavor that will be the hit of the party.

Will make 12-16 large stuffed mushrooms. Experiment with other fillings as well. Delicious!!

Herb Encrusted Grouper
Charlie

1 8 oz. Grouper filet
2 shallots
2 egg yolks
2 cups oil
2 tsp. fresh thyme, chopped and divided
2 cups panko (Japanese bread crumbs)
Lawry's Seasoning Salt and Mrs. Dash's original season
    ing mix
1 tbsp. fresh lemon juice
1 tsp. fresh basil and parsley
Egg wash

To make citrus aioli place shallots, egg yolks and 1 tsp. thyme in blender. Put on high setting, and slowly add oil until mixture becomes thick. Add lemon juice, salt and pepper; set aside. Mix together bread crumbs, 1 tsp. thyme, basil and parsley. Dredge grouper in egg wash, then coat with herb crust. Sauté on both sides

until golden brown, then bake at 350° for 10 to 12 minutes, until firm.

Serve with citrus aioli on the side.

Herbed New Potatoes
Charlie

12 small new potatoes
4 tsp. butter
4 teaspoons minced fresh parsley
4 teaspoons minced fresh chives
Fresh parsley sprigs for garnish

Peel ½ inch strip around the center of each potato and immediately place potatoes in a medium saucepan of cold water.

Add enough additional water to the saucepan to covet the potatoes by 2 inches. Bring to a boil over medium-high heat. Boil until the potatoes are easily pierced by a fork but firm, about 20 minutes; drain. Do not overcook. Cover to keep warm.

Place the butter in a microwave-safe bowl. Microwave on High until melted, about 5 to 10 seconds. Stir in minced parsley and chives. Pour the butter mixture over the potatoes and toss to coat.

Spoon the potatoes into a serving bowl. Garnish with springs of parsley.
Serve immediately.

For variety, sprinkle with chopped cooked bacon and/or finely minced green onions.

Parmigiano Regiano Crusted Pork Tenderloin
Charlie

I lb. pork tenderloin, trimmed of fat and silver skin
¼ cup Panko bread crumbs*
2 tbls. Parmigiano Regiano cheese, grated
2 tbsp. canola oil
I small Vidalia onion, chopped
2 cloves garlic, minced
Coarse salt and freshly ground black pepper

Cut tenderloin into 8 slices about I inch thick. Place each slice on a clean, hard surface and flatten with a meat mallet to ½ inch thickness. Using a medium bowl, combine breadcrumbs and cheese, seasoned with salt and pepper. Dredge pork slices to coat. Using a large sauté pan over medium heat, add the oil. Sauté onions stirring frequently until tender, about 5 minutes. Add garlic and cook until fragrant, about I minute. Using a slotted spoon, remove onion and garlic, set aside. Increase heat to medium high and cook tenderloin, until cooked through, about 3 minutes per side. Serve pork topped with sautéed onions and garlic.

*Panko breadcrumbs are Japanese, and if you can't find them in your grocery store, try an Asian market. I usually buy all they have when I find it.

Petits Pois
Charlie

2 tbls. green onion with tops, chopped
1/3 cup butter
I cup Boston lettuce, chopped
2 tbls. parsley, snipped
½ tsp. sugar

¼ tsp. salt
Dash of pepper
2 6 oz. cans tiny green peas, drained

In saucepan cook onions in butter till tender, but not brown. Add lettuce, parsley, sugar, salt and pepper. Cook until lettuce is wilted. Stir in peas; heat through. Serves 6.

Pork Chops with Caramelized Onions
Charlie

6 tbls. vegetable oil
8 center cut rib pork chops, each about 8 oz. (I inch thick)
I cup plus 5 tbls. all purpose flour
I tsp. plus I tbl. Hungarian sweet paprika
8 cups sliced onions, (about 4 large)
I tsp. Sugar
4 tsp. minced garlic
4 cups canned beef broth
¾ cup grated smoked Gouda cheese with rind, (about 3 oz.)
3 tbls. Butter
Mrs. Dash original seasoning
Lawry's seasoning salt

Preheat oven to 350°. Heat 3 tablespoons oil in heavy large skillet over high heat. Season pork with Mrs. Dash seasoning and Lawry's seasoning salt. Dredge in I cup flour; shake off excess. Working in batches, add pork to skillet and sauté until brown about 3 minutes per side. Arrange pork in single layer in 15x10x2 inch glass baking dish. Sprinkle I teaspoon paprika over pork.

Discard contents of skillet; wipe clean. Add 3 tablespoons oil; heat over medium high heat. Add onions;

sprinkle with sugar and sauté until well browned, stirring often, about 20 minutes. Add garlic; sauté 1 minute. Add 1 tablespoon paprika. Place onions over pork. Pour enough broth over meat so that chops are almost covered. Cover with foil. Bake until pork is tender, about 45 minutes. (Can be made 1 day ahead. Uncover; cool slightly. Cover; chill. Rewarm covered pork in 350° oven, about 20 minutes.)
Reduce oven temperature to 200°. Using tongs, transfer pork to large bowl, leaving onion mixture in baking dish. Pour contents of baking dish into strainer set over medium bowl. Return onion mixture to same baking dish, spreading evenly (reserve cooking liquid). Arrange pork a top onions; sprinkle cheese. Cover dish with foil; set in oven to keep warm.

Melt butter in heavy large saucepan over medium heat. Add 5 tablespoons flour. Cook, until mixture just begins to color, whisking often (mixture will be dry and crumbly), about 4 minutes. Gradually whisk in reserved cooking liquid. Bring sauce to boil, whisking constantly. Boil until thickened, whisking often, about 5 minutes. Season with Mrs. Dash original and Lawry's seasoning salt.

Transfer pork and onions to plates. Spoon sauce around pork and serve.
Serves 8.

Roast Pork with Rosemary
Charlie

4 lbs. pork loin roast, shank bone in
10 cloves garlic; peeled and mashed
3 tbsp. dried rosemary
1 tbsp. salt
1 tbsp. coarse ground black pepper
2 tbsp. olive or salad oil

Place roast on rack in shallow roasting pan. Insert meat thermometer in thickest part of the roast, but not touching the bone. *

Mix the garlic, rosemary, pepper and oil. Rub evenly over the meat. Let stand at room temperature 1 1/2 to 2 hours.
Roast uncovered at 325 degrees for 1 1/2 hours or until meat temperature reaches 150 degrees. Increase over temperature to 400 degrees. Roast 10 to 15 minutes longer until temperature reaches 175 degrees. Cover.

Let rest 20 to 30 minutes before carving. This is good served with rice and steamed broccoli or cauliflower.

*If you don't have a temperature gauge that will go in oven that is ok. But you should check the temperature after cooking.

Scalloped Potatoes with Sweet Vidalia Onions
Charlie

4 medium potatoes, peeled & sliced
2 medium Vidalia onions, thinly sliced
1 cup butter milk
1 tbsp. fresh parsley
Salt and pepper to taste
Bread crumbs (Panko if you can find it)
1 cup grated Cheddar cheese

Place potatoes in pot, cover with water, and cook until tender. Cool potatoes, peel and slice. Place 1 layer in buttered casserole dish. Place layer of onion. Mix buttermilk, sour cream and seasonings. Pour over layers. Place another layer of potatoes, then onions. Pour remaining milk mixture over layers. Sprinkle bread

crumbs over top of casserole.
Bake for 20 minutes in 350° oven. Remove from oven, sprinkle grated cheese on top of bread crumbs. Return to oven and cook for 10 minutes or until cheese melts.

Seasoned Rice Pilaf
Charlie

2 tbsp. butter
2 tbsp. onions, chopped
1 ½ cup chicken broth
1 cup instant rice, uncooked
½ bay leaf
½ tsp. thyme
2 dashes Tabasco
Mrs. Dash, to taste
½ tsp. Lawry's seasoning salt

Preheat oven to 450°. Melt butter in a large saucepan, add onion and cook for 2 or 3 minutes over medium heat. Add broth, rice and seasonings. Increase heat. Bring mixture to a boil. Remove from heat and put all into a 1 ½ quart baking dish. Bake uncovered at 450° for 17 minutes. Remove bay leaf and serve.

Smothered Chicken Breast
Charlie

5 tbsp. olive oil, divided
2 large onions, peeled, sliced, and separated into rings
8 oz. fresh mushrooms, sliced
6 boneless, skinless, chicken breast halves *
2/3 cup all-purpose flour, divided
½ tsp. salt
½ tsp. ground white pepper
2 cups fat-free chicken broth
¼ cup capers, drained
½ red bell pepper, chopped

In a large nonstick skillet, heat 1 tablespoon olive oil over medium-high heat. Add the onions and cook until golden brown stirring occasionally. Remove from skillet and set aside.

Add 1 tablespoon of oil to the same skillet and cook the mushrooms for 3 to 5 minutes. Set aside in the same bowl with the onions.

Place 1 chicken breast between two pieces of plastic wrap or wax paper. Lightly pound the chicken with the flat side of a mallet or rolling pin until it is ½ inch thick. Remove the wrap. Repeat until all the chicken has been flattened. Cut each breast in half.

Combine 1/3 cup flour, salt and pepper in a flat dish. Dip each side of chicken breast in flour mixture to coat. Heat 2 tablespoons oil in skillet over medium-high heat. Brown chicken lightly on both sides. Arrange chicken in one layer in 13x9 inch baking dish. Top with onions and mushrooms.

Add remaining 1/3 cup flour and remaining 1 tablespoon olive oil to skillet and stir until all the flour is absorbed. Add chicken broth and stir until smooth. Cook over medium-high heat until mixture boils and thickens to form gravy. Stir in the capers.

Pour the sauce over the chicken and vegetables. Bake in a 375° oven for 25 minutes or until the chicken is cooked all the way through. Sprinkle with chopped red bell pepper.

* I prefer to buy chicken with skin and bone and prepare it myself. It seems to keep its moisture better.

Southern Fried Catfish
Charlie

1 cup of buttermilk
2/3 cups of beer, I use Miller Lite
8 catfish fillets, about 4 ounces each
1 cup cornmeal
1 cup all purpose flour
½ cup cornstarch
1 tbsp. paprika
2 tbsp. Lawry's Seasoning Salt, or to your taste
2 tbsp. Mrs. Dash Original Seasoning, or to your taste
Peanut oil, for pan frying

Mix buttermilk with beer in large glass bowl. Add catfish and marinate in the refrigerator for 2 hours, but no longer than that.

Mix cornmeal, flour, cornstarch, paprika, salt and pepper in a small bowl. Mix well.
Drain catfish and discard marinade. Toss fillets lightly, one at a time in breading mixture to coat them. Place breaded fish carefully on a large baking sheet lined with wax paper, making sure fillets don't touch one another. Refrigerate for 30 minutes.

Heat oven to 200°. Pour peanut oil 2 inches deep in a heavy skillet. Heat oil to 355° (check temperature with a frying thermometer). Slowly add fillets two at a time, frying them for about 2 ½ minutes on each side, or just until they are golden brown.

Remove each fillet with a slotted spoon and place it on a paper towel to drain. Once the fillet has been drained, transfer it o a patter, and keep warm in oven until all the fillets have been fried. Work quickly so fish doesn't get overdone. Serve immediately.

I think the base of this recipe came from Louis Osteen of Pawley's Island.

Spicy Aioli
Charlie

¼ cup lemon juice
3 garlic cloves
2 egg yolks
1 tsp. fresh minced ginger
1 tsp. ground cumin
½ tsp. cayenne pepper
½ tsp. paprika
1 tsp. kosher salt
½ tsp. fresh ground pepper
½ cup cold water
1 ½ cups olive oil

Put lemon juice, garlic, egg yolks, ginger and spices in a blender, process until well mixed-about 30 seconds.

Add water and mix well.

With blender running, slowly add the oil in a slow, steady stream until it has been incorporated. You should end up with a creamy, mayonnaise like sauce.

Note: This is great for dipping nearly anything in— shrimp, crab cakes, crudités, fritters or anything else.

Spinach Dip
Charlie

1 package frozen spinach, thawed and drained
1 package frozen artichokes, chopped
1 small can green chilies
1 cup mayonnaise
1/3 cup Parmesan cheese, grated
1 cup Monterey Jack cheese, coarsely grated
2 cloves garlic, minced

Thaw and squeeze spinach, using cheesecloth or strainer. Combine ingredients reserving ¼ cup of Monterey Jack cheese. Put the spinach mixture into a baking dish and sprinkle on the reserved ¼ cup of Jack cheese. Bake at 350° in preheated oven until top bubbles.

Serve with vegetable sticks, sour dough bread or tortilla chips.

Strawberry Desert
Charlie

This recipe came from the Strawberry Festible in my home town of Reynolds, Ga.

    2 cups water
    2 cups sugar
    5 tbs. Cornstarch
    Dash salt
    1 tbs. Lemon Juice
    1- 3 oz. pkg. strawberry jello
    Strawberries (about 3 small baskets)

Crust:

    1 cup margarine or butter, melted
    1 cup pecans, chopped
    2 cups self-rising flour

For the crust mix the above and press in a 9x12 pan or pyrex. Bake for 10-12 minutes at 350° until light brown. (May need to cook a little longer). Cool crust. Put sliced strawberries over crust. Need to be several slices thick.

For filling cook water, sugar and cornstarch, lemon juice and a dash of salt until thickened. Remove from heat, add jello and stir. Let cool, not completely, but not hot to the touch. If you wait too long, it will begin to gel. Pour cooled filling over crust with strawberries.